W9-AFX-164

6/17

LEADING WOMEN

Ellen DeGeneres

Television
Comedian
and Gay
Rights Activist

KATE SHOUP

Cavendish
Square
New York

TALCOTT
LIBRARY

Published in 2017 by Cavendish Square Publishing, LLC
243 5th Avenue, Suite 136, New York, NY 10016

Copyright © 2017 by Cavendish Square Publishing, LLC

First Edition

No part of this publication may be reproduced, stored in a retrieval system, or transmitted in any
form or by any means—electronic, mechanical, photocopying, recording, or otherwise—without the
prior permission of the copyright owner. Request for permission should be addressed to Permissions,
Cavendish Square Publishing, 243 5th Avenue, Suite 136, New York, NY 10016. Tel (877) 980-4450;
fax (877) 980-4454.

Website: cavendishsq.com

This publication represents the opinions and views of the author based on his or her personal
experience, knowledge, and research. The information in this book serves as a general guide only. The
author and publisher have used their best efforts in preparing this book and disclaim liability rising
directly or indirectly from the use and application of this book.

CPSIA Compliance Information: Batch #CS16CSQ

All websites were available and accurate when this book was sent to press.

Library of Congress Cataloging-in-Publication Data

Names: Shoup, Kate, 1972- author.
Title: Ellen DeGeneres : television comedian and gay rights activist / Kate
Shoup.
Description: New York : Cavendish Square Publishing, [2016] | Series: Leading
women | Includes bibliographical references and index.
Identifiers: LCCN 2016006893 (print) | LCCN 2016010590 (ebook)
ISBN 9781502619891 (library bound) | ISBN 9781502619907 (ebook)
Subjects: LCSH: DeGeneres, Ellen--Juvenile literature. | Comedians--United
States--Biography--Juvenile literature. | Television personalities--United
States--Biography--Juvenile literature.
Classification: LCC PN2287.D358 S56 2016 (print) | LCC PN2287.D358 (ebook)
DDC 792.702/8092--dc23
LC record available at http://lccn.loc.gov/2016006893

Editorial Director: David McNamara
Editor: Elizabeth Schmermund
Copy Editor: Rebecca Rohan
Art Director: Jeffrey Talbot
Designer: Stephanie Flecha
Production Assistant: Karol Szymczuk
Photo Research: J8 Media

The photographs in this book are used by permission and through the courtesy of: Joe Seer/
Shutterstock.com, cover, 1; Seth Poppel Photo Yearbook Library, 4, 12; Ron Galella, Ltd./WireImage/
Getty Images, 11, 16, 32; The LIFE PictureCollection/Getty Images, 18, 27, 31; Steve Allen/The
Image Bank/Getty Images, 25; © Moviestore collection Ltd Alamy Stock Photo, 39; Julie Alissi/
J8 Media, 39, 58; Mirek Towski/DMI/The LIFE Picture Collection/Getty Images, 46; Monty
Brinton/CBS/Getty Images, 50; Cliff Lipson/CBS/Getty Images, 56; Jeff Vespa/WireImage for
Harrison & Shriftman/Getty Images, 61; JAMAL A. WILSON/AFP/Getty Images, 62; Lara
Porzak Photography/Getty Images, 66; Frazer Harrison/Getty Images, 70; Craig Greenhill/Newspix/
Getty Images, 72; Dave Kotinsky/Getty Images, 76; Frederick M. Brown/Getty Images, 78; Ellen
DeGeneres/Twitter/Getty Images, 82; Neil Rasmus/BFA/Sipa USA/Newscom, 88.

Printed in the United States of America

CONTENTS

CHAPTER ONE

Ellen's Early Years

When Ellen Lee DeGeneres was born on January 26, 1958, her parents no doubt believed she was a special child. Just how special DeGeneres was, however, they would not realize until later. Indeed, based on their own humble backgrounds—her father, Elliott, sold insurance and her mother, Betty, worked as an administrative assistant— there was no reason to believe that DeGeneres would grow up to become one of America's most beloved (and, for a time, controversial) comics!

Even as Ellen DeGeneres grew older, there was little to suggest that she would grow up to be a famous comedian, least of all to DeGeneres herself. "I was

A teenage Ellen DeGeneres poses with her high school tennis team.

obsessed with animals, and I really thought I'd join the Peace Corps or go to Africa and study apes or be a veterinarian," DeGeneres recalls. Still, DeGeneres would watch comics on *The Ed Sullivan Show* with fascination as a young child. "[But it] must have been a subconscious thing because at that time I had no idea that I wanted to be a comic," she wrote.

If anyone in the family were to achieve such a feat, it was widely assumed it would be DeGeneres's brother Vance. Four years her senior, Vance was considered the humorous one in the family.

Ellen's Royal Roots

Although DeGeneres's immediate family was of modest means, her family tree boasts some very wealthy branches. In 2011, thanks to a genealogical search, DeGeneres discovered that she is fifteenth cousins with Kate Middleton, Duchess of Cambridge and future queen of England. The two women share a common ancestor: Thomas Fairfax. As DeGeneres quipped in her book *Seriously ... I'm Kidding*, this revelation "makes it a lot less weird that I have everyone who works for me call me Your Royal Highness." Based on this newfound information, a cheeky DeGeneres lobbied hard for an invitation to the Royal Wedding, but, sadly, she was rebuffed.

Ellen's Early Childhood

Ellen DeGeneres spent her early child in Metairie, Louisiana, a suburb of New Orleans, noted for its aboveground cemeteries. According to Kathleen Tracy, author of *Ellen: The Real Story of Ellen DeGeneres*, her father Elliott was "steady and reliable, someone who could be considered a solid family man." Elliott was also a devout Christian Scientist.

In her book *My Point … And I Do Have One*, DeGeneres writes,

> I was raised a Christian Scientist and was taught to believe that we could heal our bodies through prayer, that sickness was an illusion that could be defeated by the power of the spirit. Since my family were Christian Scientists, we probably saved a bundle: no aspirin, no medicine at all." She went on to quip, "I didn't take my first aspirin until I was in my teens and even now I feel a twinge of guilt when I go to the pharmacy.

Ellen at School

When DeGeneres was in the third grade, her family moved to Audubon Park, a New Orleans neighborhood about five miles north of the famous French Quarter. But they would not stay put for long. Indeed, the DeGeneres family moved several times during Ellen's childhood—and that often meant she was forced to start over at a new school. DeGeneres recalls, "When I was a kid, we moved around so much … It was weird being the new kid in school all the time." This took its toll. "I always wanted people to like me," she said. "I wanted to feel like I belonged." Given her seemingly permanent "outsider" status, it's no surprise that DeGeneres did not care for school.

DeGeneres disliked school for another reason, too: She had a short attention span and couldn't pretend to be interested in subjects that weren't appealing to her. There was no doubt DeGeneres was keenly intelligent. But when it came to school, she lacked the motivation to excel.

Ellen's Parents Split

In 1972, after twenty years of marriage, DeGeneres's parents got a divorce. DeGeneres, then fourteen years old, moved with her mother back to Metairie, although she still saw her father on a regular basis. Her beloved brother Vance, who was eighteen and already working a job at a radio station, moved out on his own.

After the divorce, DeGeneres's mother, Betty, was depressed. In her attempts to cheer her mother up, DeGeneres discovered she had a gift for comedy. "I was helping [my mother] cope with a broken heart. It brought us closer together and made me realize the power of humor," she said.

During this hard time, DeGeneres realized that making her mother laugh actually helped Betty recover from the pain of her divorce. "To be able, as a child, to make your mother, who you look up to, change her mood from depression to one of so much happiness is a very powerful thing," DeGeneres once said. She added, "To know that I could make my mom feel good started pushing me toward comedy."

DeGeneres discovered something else, too: she no longer identified as a Christian Scientist. As she grew older, she left her father's religion farther and farther behind. "And if you want me to prove it," DeGeneres once joked, "I'll take an aspirin right now."

Ellen Uprooted

In 1974, Betty remarried. Her new husband, Roy Gressendorf, worked for the electric company. Unfortunately, DeGeneres and her stepfather did not see eye to eye. Gressendorf did not approve of DeGeneres, who had grown rebellious and had started spending more and more time with friends away from home. Gressendorf also frowned on DeGeneres's lack of motivation with regard to school.

In an attempt to set her straight, DeGeneres's mother and stepfather decided to move to Atlanta, Texas, a town of just six thousand people situated twenty-five miles south of Texarkana. They found a charming old house on Taylor Street and enrolled her in the local high school,

Ellen's Big Brother

Although Ellen DeGeneres would eventually become the most famous member of her family, her brother, Vance, also enjoyed a certain level of fame—particularly around the family's hometown of New Orleans. During the late 1970s, Vance hosted a popular radio program, *New Wave New Orleans*, and played bass guitar in a local band called The Cold.

Vance also worked on several short films. The most famous of these was *Mr. Bill*, a series of short films that aired on *Saturday Night Live*. These films featured a claymation clown named Mr. Bill, who, along with his dog, Spot, routinely suffered various indignities and abuse by "Mr. Hands" (actually Vance's hands). In each film, Mr. Bill wound up crushed, squashed, dismembered, or worse. Mr. Bill's high-pitched "Ohhh nooooooo!"—which he cried out each time he was injured—became a catch phrase of sorts.

In 1999, Vance began a two-year stint as a correspondent on the popular show, *The Daily Show with Jon Stewart.* He was perhaps best known for his "Tale of Survival" series, in which he reported trivial incidents in the style of a *Dateline NBC* report. While at the *Daily Show,* Vance worked with Steve Carell, another correspondent. Carell parlayed his work at *The Daily Show* into a successful film career and, in 2008, launched his own production company, Carousel Productions. Today, Vance—who married Scottish actress Joanne Brooks in 2013—runs Carousel Productions, developing comedy movies alongside his old friend Carell.

Ellen DeGeneres with her big brother Vance at the 1995 Golden Globe Awards

Atlanta High. For DeGeneres, it was a culture shock to move from such a large city to a small town.

DeGeneres tried to make the best of things. She made friends. She sang in the chorus. She played varsity tennis, winning the Outstanding Player Award her first year. She even had a boyfriend, Ben Heath, who was a football star and top student. Blond, tall, and handsome, Ben was "smitten with Ellen's sense of humor." DeGeneres once admitted in an interview to almost getting married to Ben in high school.

Still, life in Texas went from bad to worse. Ellen's mother Betty discovered a lump in her breast, which turned out to be cancerous. Betty quickly underwent treatment for breast cancer. This was during a time when no one spoke of the disease. "Everything was a dirty

little secret back then," DeGeneres recalls. "The fact that she had a mastectomy was not spoken of. She tried to shield me from it a little bit, but she needed my help with recovery and physical rehabilitation. It bonded us even more."

DeGeneres's senior portrait

As Betty underwent treatment, Ellen experienced something even worse: Her stepfather molested her. Gressendorf told Ellen that he thought he felt a lump in Betty's other breast, but he didn't want to alarm Betty, so he needed to feel Ellen's to "make sure." Gressendorf then made his stepdaughter "lie down, because he said he felt [Betty's] while she was lying down." In another incident, Gressendorf tried to break down DeGeneres's bedroom door. She "had to kick a window out and escape and sleep in a hospital all night long." At first, DeGeneres told no one. After a few years, however, she shared her secret with Betty, who eventually left Gressendorf. Finally, in 2005, DeGeneres went public with the story. "It's important for teenage girls out there to hear that there are different ways to say no," DeGeneres explained. "And if it ever happens to them, they should tell someone right away."

Ellen Leaves the Nest

Not surprisingly, DeGeneres could not leave home soon enough. The day after she graduated from Atlanta High in May of 1976, DeGeneres packed up her yellow Volkswagen and left town. Her destination: New Orleans, where she moved in with her grandmother.

Although she had not planned to attend college, DeGeneres did enroll at the University of New Orleans. "I hated school, but I started college because everyone else was going," said DeGeneres. But she soon dropped out. "I just remember sitting there and they were talking about the history of Greek theater or something and thinking, 'This is not what I want to know.'"

Adrift, DeGeneres landed a series of odd jobs. She did clerical work at a law firm. She sold clothes. She wrapped packages at a department store. She kept the books for a wig store. She washed cars. She painted houses. She mowed lawns. She worked as a bartender, and then as a waitress. She sold vacuum cleaners. "Boy, did that job suck," DeGeneres later joked. All the while, she moved from one flea-ridden apartment to the next.

Struggles with Her Sexuality

Finding meaningful work was just one of DeGeneres's problems. Perhaps more pressing was her struggle to find *herself*.

DeGeneres was confused about her sexuality. During her time in Texas, she had her first sexual experience with a girl. Still, she did not believe she was gay. "I didn't think about it as being gay," DeGeneres said. "I thought it was just her." She noted, "I dated guys. I liked guys." But, she added, "I knew that I liked girls, too." For a while, DeGeneres tried to just ignore her feelings.

Some people recognize their sexuality early on. Others are slower to identify this aspect of themselves. DeGeneres fell into the latter category and was shocked at first. Eventually, she began to understand that she was attracted to women. By the time she was in her early twenties, she was clear on her sexual identity.

Soon, DeGeneres shared this information with her mother. In order to better understand, Betty went to the library to read up about homosexuality. In time, she began to understand her daughter's sexuality. DeGeneres's father, Elliott—with whom she was living at the time—had a different reaction. "[My father and stepmother] asked me to move out of the house," DeGeneres recalled. "They just thought it would be better for me to live somewhere else because the woman he married had two daughters." She added, "They didn't want that to be around her little girls." In time, Elliott saw things differently and admitted that he had been wrong.

Ellen Finds Her Calling

All that was left was for DeGeneres to find her way professionally. She saw her brother Vance—who by then had become somewhat of a local celebrity in New Orleans—as an example. "Everybody knew who he was," DeGeneres later told *People*. "That's what motivated me to do something, because I watched him get all this attention and glory."

In 1980, when she was twenty-two years old, a friend asked her to do a stand-up routine at a local benefit. According to DeGeneres, an organization needed to raise money but wasn't able to find a celebrity who could help them out, so they asked her to tell jokes. The problem? DeGeneres didn't have any material. But she quickly came up with an idea. "I always thought it was funny

Ellen DeGeneres

DeGeneres on stage, early in her stand-up career

when people have something to tell you, and they take a huge bite out of something, and then they make you wait to finish that bite," she said. So that's what she did. She got onstage and said, "I gotta tell you about the funniest thing that happened to me the other day." Then she pulled out a Burger King Whopper and took a huge bite. "I'd finish that, then start a new sentence, take another huge bite … and by the time I finished everything, I looked at my watch and said, 'Oh, my time is up. Gotta go.' Then I left. I'd gotten maybe ten words out."

The audience loved it. DeGeneres's act was met with thunderous applause. Afterward, someone approached her and asked her to do a show at a coffeehouse nearby. DeGeneres said yes … and then promptly freaked out. What would she do onstage? Then she remembered something: For the past few months, she'd been writing short humor pieces. She had considered submitting them to magazines for publication, but had yet to do so. Those pieces could serve as the basis of her stand-up act.

Emboldened, she performed a set at the coffeehouse. Again, she was a hit … and she made fifteen dollars. Soon, she was performing at small venues all over New Orleans. Finally, Ellen DeGeneres had found her way!

TALCOTT
LIBRARY

CHAPTER TWO

From Tragedy to Triumph

The year 1980 was an exciting time for Ellen DeGeneres. Not only had she found her calling—stand-up comedy—but she was also in love. The object of DeGeneres's affections was a chipper blonde named Kat Perkoff, whom she had known for some time. According to Kat's sister Rachel, Kat was a talented writer and a local icon. Soon, DeGeneres and Perkoff moved in together. DeGeneres believed she had found the woman with whom she would spend the rest of her life.

A young Ellen DeGeneres, ready to take over the world of stand-up comedy

Love and Loss

Then, tragedy struck. On June 26, 1980, Kat was killed in a car accident. According to her sister Rachel, she "died in a white Mercedes after it veered off a highway, hit a concrete bridge support, and split cleanly in half." Incredibly, on her way home from a club where her brother's band was playing, DeGeneres witnessed the aftermath of the accident, but she had no idea that Perkoff was in the car. "It was split in two, and we heard sirens behind us, so it had just happened. Nobody was there yet. We just kept going." It was not until the next morning that DeGeneres discovered Perkoff had been killed in the crash. It was another shock for DeGeneres— one that would change the course of her life. In an interview, DeGeneres admitted that she felt guilty for not being with Perkoff that night: "I felt all kinds of things. I felt responsible. I felt how fragile life is."

"Phone Call to God"

Shortly after the accident, a despondent DeGeneres found herself living alone in a flea-ridden apartment. (She had been forced to move from the apartment she had shared with Perkoff, unable to afford the rent on her own.) "I remember thinking, 'It just seems so ridiculous that this young, 23-year-old girl who I was just living with [is] gone, and fleas are here,'" DeGeneres recalls. "I thought, 'It would be great to just pick up the phone and call up God and talk about this.'"

Suddenly, her brain kicked into high gear. What would happen, she mused, if you actually *could* pick up the phone and call God? She put pen to paper and, in a matter of minutes, she had written an entire **monologue,** or **bit,** called "Phone Call to God."

DeGeneres began the bit by observing that everything on Earth exists for a reason … except fleas. She then said, "At times like this, when we can't figure it out for ourselves, wouldn't it be great if we could just pick up the phone and call up God and ask Him these things?" Next, she would pretend to call God. When God answered, the audience heard DeGeneres's side of the conversation.

"Yeah, hi God. This is Ellen. Ellen DeGeneres. DeGeneres. What's so funny? No, I never thought of that. It does sound like that, doesn't? I get it. Listen," DeGeneres continued. "If you weren't too busy—sure, I'll hold on." She would then pretend to cover the receiver with her hand and explain to the audience, "Someone's at the gate."

DeGeneres would wait a moment, looking off into the distance. Then she began singing the hymn "Onward Christian Soldiers." Finally, God would return to the line. "Yeah," DeGeneres said. "Just singing along to your tape. It's not a tape? They're good! They're great."

Finally, she posed her question to God. "Listen," she said. "There are certain things on this Earth I just don't understand why they're here. No, not Charo. But there are certain things. Like insects. No, bees are great. The honey. That was clever. I was thinking more about fleas. They seem to have no benefit—"

Here, God interrupted DeGeneres. She pretended to listen for a moment, then said, "No, I didn't realize how many people were employed by the flea collar industry. Not to mention sprays. Well. Yeah, I guess you're right. Of course you are! Of course you are. Being who you are."

Next, God sneezed. "Oh!" said DeGeneres. "You got a little cold. God bless you. Or bless yourself! Bless yourself! Yeah, I'm still doing that comedy."

"Oh, you have a joke for me," she said next. "I'd love to hear it. Uh-huh. No, I got time. Of course you would know that more than me, huh! Joke. Go ahead." She pretended to listen intently. "Who's there?" she said. Again, she listened. "God who?" Finally, the punchline: "Godzilla! Oh, you're incredibly funny! Yeah! Oh, another one. Sure." Again, it was a knock-knock joke. "Who's there? … God who? … Gotta dime!" DeGeneres continued, "Oh! Oh, no, I don't have time for another one. No. Yeah, I just remembered an appointment I have to get to so I gotta go. How about that? God who? Gotta go? Cute? Stupid."

Finally, it was time to wrap it up. "Alrighty," DeGeneres said. "It was good talking to you too. I'll talk to you later."

When she finished writing the bit, DeGeneres knew that it was not only funny, but that it would become an

Johnny Carson's Couch

Who was Johnny Carson? And what was the significance of being invited to sit on his couch?

Johnny Carson was the host of the popular late-night show *The Tonight Show Starring Johnny Carson* from 1962 to 1992. Among other things, Carson was known for featuring up-and-coming comics on his show. For comics like DeGeneres, landing a spot on *The Tonight Show* was like finding Willy Wonka's golden ticket. It allowed them to perform in front of millions of viewers and was often the launching pad for their entire careers.

Typically, after a comic finished performing on *The Tonight Show*, Johnny would clap and cut to commercial. But if he *really* liked a comic's routine, he would invite that person to come sit on his couch. In time, "sitting on Johnny's couch" became shorthand for "making it as a comic."

Incredibly, in all his years as host of *The Tonight Show*—by this time, in 1980, he'd held that position for some 18 years—Johnny had never invited a female comic to sit on his couch. DeGeneres was determined to be the first.

instant success. She noted, "I read it and said, 'I'm going to do that on Johnny Carson one day. And he's going to love it. And he's going to invite me to sit on the couch.'"

With "Phone Call to God," DeGeneres turned tragedy into triumph. She later said that while it was a very trying time, the ability to make jokes from this tragedy put her on "a better path." DeGeneres explained, "I could have just gone out and gotten drunk every night, and spiraled out and just felt sorry for myself, and become a rebel. I went the other way. I decided I wanted to figure things out. I wanted to find out what all this is about."

Clyde's Comedy Corner

Even as she improved her skills as a comic, DeGeneres still lacked an outlet for her art. There was no dedicated comedy club in New Orleans. Although she spent the majority of her time writing material, she couldn't reasonably view comedy as a viable career choice.

In December of 1980, all that changed. A comedy club opened in New Orleans—the first one to open up in the city. Clyde's Comedy Corner was the only club where local comics could perform. The owner, Clyde Abercrombie, quickly hired DeGeneres to perform one show a night during the week and two a night on Fridays and Saturdays. Even better, she was paid to perform. "I was getting paid like three hundred dollars a week, enough so that I didn't have to work a regular job," DeGeneres recalls.

Working at Clyde's Comedy Corner was an incredible learning opportunity. "I learned what it was all about by on-the-job training," DeGeneres said. Specifically, she learned how to engage her audience and to deliver her jokes slowly and with the greatest possible effect. She also learned to stay true to herself.

The site of Clyde's Comedy Corner, where Ellen learned the art of stand-up.

At first, DeGeneres served as the **opener.** It's the opener's job to warm the audience up. In time, she was promoted to the middle spot. By late 1981, DeGeneres had claimed the closing act and was also the show's **emcee.**

Clyde's Comedy Corner also hosted comics from outside New Orleans. After seeing her act, these headliners told DeGeneres she was a good comic and that she should try her stand-up in a big city like New York or Los Angeles. Inspired by their encouragement—and by a friend who had moved to San Francisco—DeGeneres took the plunge and moved to the Bay Area.

Unfortunately, things did not go well. None of the clubs in San Francisco were terribly interested in featuring a comic whose sole claim to fame was emceeing at a comedy club in New Orleans. "I loved San Francisco," DeGeneres said of her brief time there. "But I didn't have any money." Eventually, she grew homesick and returned to New Orleans. Unfortunately, by the time she returned, Clyde's Comedy Corner had shut down. "Suddenly, I'm out of comedy," DeGeneres said about this frustrating period in her career.

"The Funniest Person in America"

Wiped out financially, DeGeneres took the first job she could find, as an office assistant. For a year, her days consisted of making copies and brewing coffee. She felt lost and frustrated. Finally, she saw a glimmer of hope: She found out about a contest sponsored by Showtime. The popular cable network wanted to find the "Funniest Person in America." To enter, all she had to do was submit a video of her routine. Quickly, she did just that.

Soon thereafter, DeGeneres—by then living in yet another flea-infested apartment—received a phone call. Showtime was calling from New York. Based on the tape she sent in, she had become one of five finalists in the competition. DeGeneres and the other finalists were invited to perform their routines in front of a panel of judges that included established comedians Soupy Sales,

Ellen DeGeneres, circa 1990

Harvey Korman, and Pee-Wee Herman. "They all picked me as the winner," DeGeneres recalled.

Being named "Funniest Person in America" was a real game-changer. "In one year, I went from making coffee for lawyers to being 1982's Funniest Person in America," she observed. Suddenly, Ellen DeGeneres realized, her future was very bright indeed.

California Calls

Determined to strike while the iron was hot, DeGeneres moved back to San Francisco. This time around, the city welcomed the "Funniest Person in America" with open arms. "It was amazing how well things worked out there," DeGeneres said. "I didn't really struggle at all. Things just clicked, and people started paying attention to me."

According to DeGeneres, at that time, San Francisco was the best place for comedy. Still, she knew that if she was really going to make it as a comic, she'd need to take her act on the road. She bought a van and traveled the country, performing in small bars and clubs. She quickly realized that she'd "have to be really, really tough-skinned, because it's hard." She noted, "There's lots of traveling, lots of being by yourself, lots of really rude drunk people." It wasn't as glamorous as people might think. Often, she wasn't in big cities, but in small towns and strip malls. Worse, there were "lots of places where, literally, the soup of the day got the top billing." She explained, "There would be a chalkboard on the sidewalk and it would say:

SOUP OF THE DAY: BROCCOLI. AND ELLEN
DEGENERES. And I'm not kidding."

For DeGeneres, these were **heady**—but exhausting—
times. She was on the road performing some 300 days
a year. Not surprisingly, this schedule took its toll on
the young comic. It was time for a change. DeGeneres
was, in the words of Kathleen Tracy, "ready to start the
transition to television, specifically some of the popular
cable comedy shows." And, Tracy notes, she had "started
getting her first itch to try her hand at acting." This
transition would enable DeGeneres to cut back on her
travel schedule. But, it would require her to move to
Los Angeles.

When Ellen Met Johnny

About a year after DeGeneres moved to Los Angeles,
in 1986, something amazing happened: At long last, she
was invited to perform on *The Tonight Show with Johnny
Carson*. DeGeneres was thrilled—and determined to make
the most of the opportunity. She remembered that day in
1980, when, in her grief over the death of her girlfriend,
she'd written "Phone Call to God." And she remembered
something else: her conviction that after she performed
that bit, Johnny would summon her to the couch.

On November 28, 1986, Ellen DeGeneres debuted
on *The Tonight Show*. Her fellow guests included a
famous comic, Joe Piscopo, who performed a Bruce
Springsteen parody, and a man named Dennis Hart, who

Ellen's Comedic Style

Ellen DeGeneres has a distinct comedic style, based on observations she makes during daily life—watching people shopping at the neighborhood drug store, riding the bus, or walking down the street. She has long stated that, if you look hard enough, you can find the humor in anything.

As a rule, DeGeneres steers clear of three topics: sex, politics, and religion. She also strives to keep her act clean and to avoid using profanity. Her comedy is good-natured and never relies on mean-spirited remarks. "Most comedy is based on getting a laugh at somebody else's expense," DeGeneres observes. "And I find that that's just a form of bullying in a major way … I want to be an example that you can be funny and be kind, and make people laugh without hurting somebody else's feelings."

was enjoying his fifteen minutes of fame for refusing to pay a parking ticket and, somehow, bringing his case all the way to the Supreme Court.

In the moments before going on stage, she was "as nervous as you can possibly be ever in your lifetime." DeGeneres added, "I could hear my heart. I thought that everyone would hear my heart in my chest." Still, she knew she was ready. She confidently stepped out from behind the curtain and began her five-minute set.

DeGeneres started her set with a few jokes about her family. "My grandma started walking five miles a day

The late, great Johnny Carson, host of *The Tonight Show*

when she was sixty. She's ninety-seven today and we don't know where the hell she is," she said. Then she segued to her signature bit—the one she'd written all those years before—"Phone Call to God."

She killed it. At the end of her set, the audience stood up and applauded. Carson loved it, too. And, just as DeGeneres had imagined, he invited her to come sit on his couch. "That's very clever and very fresh," Carson told her before offering her an "open invitation" to return to the show. This was an amazing moment for the aspiring comedian.

DeGeneres's performance on *The Tonight Show* was a turning point. "The fact that he wanted me to sit down and talk to him, it catapulted my career," she later said. But that wasn't the real reason why she had wanted to sit on Johnny Carson's couch. Instead, DeGeneres recalls, "I wanted to do it because I knew he would appreciate it, I knew it was smart, I knew it was different, and I knew that nobody else was doing what I was doing." She added, "That's all I wanted. I wanted people to *get* me."

CHAPTER THREE

Ellen Goes Big Time

E llen DeGeneres's 1986 appearance on *The Tonight Show with Johnny Carson* was the first of many. She would appear on the show five more times before Carson's retirement in 1992. Still, her first appearance on Carson's show was special because it started DeGeneres on the path to fame—and allowed her to make the jump to television.

Unfortunately, that jump did not occur as smoothly—or as quickly—as she would have liked. Finally, in 1989, three years after her appearance on *The Tonight Show*, DeGeneres was cast in a supporting role in a new **sitcom**, called *Open House*. She played Margo Van Meter, a

DeGeneres poses with her first book in 1995.

scatterbrained receptionist at a real estate office. It was a very small part, but DeGeneres was excited to be on television. Unfortunately, the show was not a success. It was canceled within a year.

Luckily, DeGeneres still had work. She performed in her own stand-up special on HBO. Besides, it wouldn't be too long before she was cast in a supporting role in another series, *Laurie Hill*, by **producers** Carol Black and Neal Marlens. Black and Marlens had a strong track record in Hollywood, having produced and written two spectacularly successful series, *The Wonder Years* and *Growing Pains*.

Certain that *Laurie Hill* would be a hit, DeGeneres—who played nurse Nancy MacIntyre—splurged on a new Mercedes. This proved to be premature. Upon its release, critics universally panned the show. Variety called it "cloddish," with "cloying writing," concluding that there was "little to laugh or cry at in *Laurie Hill*, despite heavy-handed attempts to elicit both reactions." *TV Guide* called it *The Blunder Years*—though the periodical did go on to praise DeGeneres, noting that she "provided desperately needed comic relief—and not enough of it." After just four episodes, network execs axed the series. Frankly, DeGeneres was relieved. She had been disappointed by her limited role. "I had so little to do it was ridiculous," she said. "I think in the pilot I had maybe two lines. I carried a folder." She added, "I was praying for it to get canceled."

These Friends of Mine

Undeterred, Black and Marlens approached DeGeneres with a new idea: developing a sitcom around her as a comedian. Black and Marlens believed DeGeneres could easily follow in the footsteps of such successful comics-turned-actors as Jerry Seinfeld, Roseanne Barr, and Tim Allen.

But DeGeneres had reservations. How would she adapt her comedy to the sitcom format? Would she be comfortable having others write her material? And there was something else that gave her pause: her sexuality. She brought this concern to Black and Marlens. "I said, 'I need to tell you something, because you may not want to create a show for me, but I'm gay. And I know that could hurt the show if it got out,'" DeGeneres recalls. "And Neal [Marlens] said, 'We know you're gay.'" And then, noted DeGeneres, Marlens said something else: "'Do you want the character to be gay?'" This idea was too much for DeGeneres, who, though out in her private life, remained closeted to the public. "I said: 'No! Absolutely not!'"

The show, called *These Friends of Mine*, would feature an ensemble cast, with DeGeneres at its center. Her character, Ellen Morgan, was, in DeGeneres's words, a "goon." As DeGeneres explained, "She tries so hard, but she's always getting into trouble."

In April 1993, the pilot episode was taped. It showcased DeGeneres's sense of humor and introduced audiences to the madcap "friends" in her life. Thrilled with the results, network execs at ABC ordered twelve more episodes.

Nearly a year later, on March 29, 1994, the first episode aired. This time, DeGeneres really *did* have a hit. *These Friends of Mine* debuted in the number seven spot in the ratings. The next episode scored even higher, landing at number three. Matt Roush of *USA Today* called the show "the warmest, smartest ABC comedy since I don't know when." *People* magazine called it "an irresistible treat."

Ellen

Despite its early success, all was not well with *These Friends of Mine*. DeGeneres quickly realized that she did not care for the direction the show—which often featured sexual situations and off-color jokes—was headed. At first, she didn't say anything. "When I first got this show, I was just so grateful, and I thought, 'Well, they know what they're doing. I should just shut up,'" she said. But soon, DeGeneres realized that she was not proud of her character on the show and didn't want her audience to think she was actually like Ellen Morgan. She explained, "All I can try to do is maintain some integrity. Even though Ellen Morgan is certainly not me, I should never say or do anything on the show I don't believe in."

And so, for the show's second season (1994–1995), DeGeneres pushed for several changes. Various actors, writers, and producers were replaced. And, perhaps most notably, the show's name was changed to *Ellen*. To help the fledgling series spread its wings, ABC execs gave it a better time slot after the popular show *Roseanne*, starring Roseanne Barr and John Goodman.

Critics took notice. Joyce Millman, TV critic for the *San Francisco Examiner*, wrote, "*Ellen* has hung in there as a genuine hit, often outranking *Roseanne*." The show finished the second season ranked thirteenth—not bad considering all the changes that had been made behind the scenes. *Ellen* was on track for a top-ten spot in the season to come.

Unfortunately, this did not come to pass. Rather, in season three (1995–1996), the show's ratings tumbled. This was no doubt due in part to larger problems at ABC; the network was on a downward spiral that would not stop until it crashed into third place behind major networks CBS and NBC. At the end of the year, the show was ranked thirty-eighth, a crushing disappointment. Network executives grasped for ideas to turn the show around. One executive suggested, rather pathetically, that Ellen Morgan adopt a puppy.

More Bad News

In 1994, Bantam Books tapped DeGeneres to write her first book—and paid her a million dollars to do so. Rather than a memoir, DeGeneres opted to write a humor book. She likened it to Woody Allen's early writing, noting, "It's going to be a mixture of a lot of things." The project proved far more taxing than DeGeneres had expected. "I'm supposed to have like sixty-thousand words or something," she said during the writing phase, "and I think I have two thousand." She continued, "Some days I feel like I have nothing to say." But, she added, "other days it just flows out of me."

The book was released in October 1995. Called *My Point ... And I Do Have One,* DeGeneres's first book debuted at number one on the *New York Times* bestseller list, although it was not well-received by critics. One critic, Lisa Schwarzbaum, wrote in *Entertainment Weekly* that "*My Point* is ... a testament to a kind of dispiriting creative threadbareness," noting that DeGeneres hobbled through it "like a novice Boston Marathoner" and grading the book at a D+. (Her later books, *The Funny Thing Is ...* and *Seriously ... I'm Kidding,* would fare better among critics.)

That same year, 1995, DeGeneres was cast in a black comedy film called *Mr. Wrong.* She was no stranger to the movies—she had appeared in two short films and a documentary, as well as making a brief appearance in *Coneheads* (1993)—but this was the first time she'd landed a lead role in a major motion picture. The movie, released in 1996, is about a young woman named Martha Alston who is looking for Mr. Right. For a time, she believes

DeGeneres with costar Bill Pullman in the 1995 film *Mr. Right*

she's found him in a man named Whitman Crawford (played by Bill Pullman). Soon, however, she realizes that Whitman is *not* Mr. Right; he is unequivocally Mr. Wrong. Martha dumps Whitman, at which point he begins stalking her in an attempt to woo her back.

The movie was about as terrible as it sounds. One critic called the film "dreadful" and "inherently unfunny." Another described it as a "sour, listless debunking of romantic comedies." It was yet another setback for the rising star.

"The Puppy Episode"

Desperate to resuscitate her show, DeGeneres considered making a major change to the character of Ellen Morgan. At a meeting with her writing staff, DeGeneres— perhaps remembering the question posed by producer Neal Marlens when she revealed to him and producer Carol Black that she was gay—asked, "What do you think if the character came out?" The writers loved the idea. Ironically, they had tossed around the very same plot twist but had been too fearful to present it to the comedian.

Ellen Morgan wouldn't be the first gay character on TV. In fact, the 1996–1997 season featured more than twenty openly gay characters, including characters on such popular shows as *Spin City*, *The Simpsons*, *Mad About You*, *Party of Five*, *Melrose Place*, *Roseanne*, and *Friends*. Gay characters had also made inroads on daytime TV, such as ABC's *All My Children*. But no network TV sitcom had ever featured a lead character who was gay.

DeGeneres and her team brought the idea to network execs. They didn't love the idea—but they didn't hate it, either. In the end, with some **trepidation**, they green-lighted the writing of the "coming out" episode—but they made no promises as to whether it would ever see the light of day. Still, it was a start.

After much back and forth, the network finally approved a script for filming in March 1997. The episode was cheekily titled "The Puppy," a reference to the network executive who had foolishly suggested that Ellen Morgan adopt a puppy to improve ratings. Rehearsals for the two-part episode started soon thereafter.

On Friday, March 14, in front of an incredibly supportive, invitation-only studio audience that included DeGeneres's mom, the episode was taped. The mood was festive, despite the fact that audience members had been subjected to a security check with metal detectors thanks to a bomb threat received by the studio. (No bombs were found, but the fact that someone would threaten to blow up the studio because of the taping of Ellen's show, featuring a gay character, was chilling.) Throughout the course of the day, the storyline—which featured several high-profile guest stars, including Billy Bob Thornton, Demi Moore, Dwight Yoakam, Gina Gershon, Kathy Najimy, k. d. lang, Melissa Etheridge, Laura Dern, and Oprah Winfrey—unfolded.

In the episode, Ellen's best friend from college, Richard, comes to town on business and invites her to dinner. During the meal, Richard's assistant, Susan, played by Laura Dern, interrupts the pair to deliver a message. Ellen and Susan register an instant liking for each other.

Later in the evening, Richard invites Ellen to his hotel room. There, to Ellen's horror, he attempts to seduce her. Ellen makes a hasty exit, only to run into Susan, who invites Ellen into *her* room. As the two chat on the couch, Ellen becomes increasingly more comfortable—until Susan says that she's gay, and that she assumes Ellen is, too. Ellen recoils. "Why would you think that?" she exclaims. "I'm not gay!" She bolts from Susan's room and goes straight back to Richard's. She knocks, and he answers, at which point Ellen kisses him and pushes him back inside the room. The next day, Ellen tells her friends about the wild and passionate night she spent with Richard.

Later in the episode, Ellen visits her therapist, played by Oprah Winfrey. During their session, Ellen recounts the *real* story of what happened with Richard: how she wasn't able to actually go through with things and had left his hotel room. Confused, Ellen admits that she just doesn't seem to "click" with men. Her therapist asks her who she *does* click with. Ellen's tentative response: "Susan."

Ellen receives word that Richard is about to leave town and assumes that Susan will be going, too. Frantic, she rushes to the airport to find them both. When she does, she apologizes to Richard. Next, she rushes to Susan and exclaims, "Okay, you were right!" Then she stalls. She can't get the words out. Frustrated, she smacks her hand on the counter—and in doing so, unwittingly switches on the PA system.

"I'm gay!" she cries. "You hear that? I'm gay! And it sounds pretty darn good!" Horrified, she realizes that she has just broadcast this information to the entire airport.

Susan smiles. "I'm proud of you," she says. "I remember how hard it was when I told my first airport full of people." Then she tells Ellen that she's not leaving with Richard after all, and the two leave the airport together.

Later, at her therapist, Ellen admits that she'd known she was gay, but just couldn't admit it to herself. "I thought if I ignored it, it would just go away," she says. Ellen continues, "I just want to be normal. I mean, you never see a cake that says, 'Good for you. You're gay.'"

Her therapist replies, "Well, then, I'll say it for you. Good for you. You're gay."

All that's left is for DeGeneres to share this news with her friends—something that, as expressed in a dream sequence that features the lion's share of guest stars, she is loath to do. But she does, and it is met with acceptance. In fact, one of the characters, Joe, makes it clear that he has won a long-standing bet about Ellen Morgan's sexuality with the others. Her friends even go so far as to organize a get-together at a nearby gay coffee shop to celebrate Ellen's coming-out. And what of Susan? During her remaining time in town, she admits to Ellen that she's in a serious relationship. Ellen is hurt but also grateful for all that Susan has done for her.

On April 30, the episode aired. Watched by some forty-two million people, it was met with rave reviews among fans and critics alike. One critic, writing for the *New York Times*, noted, "If last night's show is any indication, the new Ellen can hardly be accused of promoting a lifestyle as much as promoting tolerance." The critic added, "If Ms. DeGeneres can sustain the quality of last night's show, she deserves to succeed." *TV Guide* would rank the episode at number thirty-five on its list of The 100 Greatest TV Episodes of All Time.

Of course, you can't please everybody. There were those who felt that the show promoted a sinful lifestyle. Reverend Fred Phelps of the controversial Westboro Baptist Church griped, "It's a sign we're on the cusp of doom, of Sodom and Gomorrah." Reverend Jerry Falwell referred to DeGeneres as "Ellen DeGenerate," ironically calling to mind DeGeneres's "Phone Call to God," in which God points out that her last name sounds like "DeGenerate." The show also suffered a loss of sponsors—namely J. C. Penney, Chrysler, and Wendy's. DeGeneres was hurt by these reactions, but she took things in stride. "Jesus, as far as I'm concerned, was nonjudgmental and taught love and acceptance," she said. "That's all I know about, and that's how I live my life."

Later that spring, DeGeneres received two Emmy nominations. One was for Outstanding Actress in a Comedy Series. The other was as a writer for "The Puppy Episode." Although the Outstanding Actress award went to Helen Hunt, DeGeneres and her writing team picked up the statuette in their category. "I accept this on behalf of all the people, and the teenagers especially, out there who think there's something wrong with them because they're gay," DeGeneres said in her acceptance speech. "Don't ever let anyone make you feel ashamed of who you are!"

DeGeneres would lead the way for many TV shows that would feature gay or lesbian leads or romantic storylines with gay characters, such as *Will & Grace*, *Desperate Housewives*, *Pretty Little Liars*, *Glee*, and *The L Word*.

Ellen Comes Out

It wasn't just Ellen Morgan who came out—Ellen DeGeneres came out, too. She always thought that she would keep her private life out of the public eye. However, as her fame grew, this became impossible.

As noted by author Kathleen Tracy, once DeGeneres's show became a hit, "Ellen had to know it was only a matter of time before her life would play out in the papers—and that it probably wouldn't be pretty." Indeed, DeGeneres's love life had long been tabloid fodder. In 1994, soon after *These Friends of Mine* first aired, DeGeneres had been the subject of a *National Enquirer* story with this embarrassing headline: "TV's newest funny girl warned: Stay out of gay bars. *These Friends of Mine* star told to watch those friends of hers." According to the story, "The show's producers told her to tone down her lifestyle in public to make her heterosexual character more believable."

By the summer of 1996, DeGeneres had had enough. "I made a decision during the summer that I wasn't going to live my life as a lie anymore," she said later. "I decided that this was not going to be something I was going to live the rest of my life ashamed of."

DeGeneres's famous *Time* magazine cover

And so, the same week that ABC aired "The Puppy Episode," in which Ellen Morgan came out, so did Ellen DeGeneres. She appeared on the cover of *Time* magazine with the words "Yep, I'm Gay," was featured on *20/20* in an interview with newswoman Diane Sawyer, and appeared on *The Oprah Winfrey Show*. "For me," she told *Time*, "this has been the most freeing experience, because people can't hurt me anymore." She explained, "I don't have to worry about somebody saying something about me or a reporter trying to find out information, because now I'm in control of it." She added, "Literally, as soon as I made this decision, I lost weight. My skin cleared up. I don't have anything to be scared of, which I think outweighs whatever else happens in my career."

Ellen and Anne

During her appearance on *Oprah*, DeGeneres divulged yet another secret: that she was in a relationship with twenty-seven-year-old actress Anne Heche. DeGeneres and Heche had met about a month before at the annual *Vanity Fair* Oscar party, which DeGeneres, having just broken up with another girlfriend, Teresa Boyd, had attended alone.

During her appearance on *Oprah*, Heche was invited to join DeGeneres onstage. Heche described to Oprah how the pair met: She caught a glimpse of DeGeneres from across a crowded room and knew, right away, that they shared a connection. She approached DeGeneres,

Anne Heche

Anne Heche (pronounced "haytch") was born on May 25, 1969, in Aurora, Ohio. Her father, Donald, was a Baptist minister and choir director. Constantly in search of work, he regularly relocated the family.

When Heche was just thirteen years old, her father passed away. It was then that she learned that he had lived a double life, posing as a businessman and engaging in homosexual affairs. As a result, he had contracted AIDS—which at that time was a mysterious and incurable disease—and died. Weeks later, Anne's older brother, Nathan, was tragically killed in a car accident. Heche later claimed it was a suicide.

Anne's mother, Nancy, moved her remaining family—daughters Susan, Abigail, and Anne, the baby of the family—to a one-bedroom apartment in Chicago. In 1987, after graduating high school, Anne moved to New York against her mother's wishes, where she landed a job as an actress on the soap opera *Another World.* She played evil twins Vicky and Marley, for which she won a Daytime Emmy and a Soap Opera Digest Award.

In 1992, Anne quit *Another World* and moved to Hollywood. She appeared in a succession of films including *The Adventures of Huck Finn* (1993), *The Juror* (1996), *Walking and Talking* (1996), *Donnie Brasco* (1997), and *Volcano* (1997), which premiered the same week as "The Puppy Episode." (Ironically, Anne had been one of the actresses considered for the role of Susan in "The Puppy Episode," but had been beaten out by Laura Dern.)

Heche and DeGeneres step out at a film premiere.

the two began chatting, and a romantic relationship was born.

Heche had historically dated only men, including musician Lindsey Buckingham and comedian Steve Martin, both twenty-plus years her senior, and was surprised by her feelings for DeGeneres. As Heche put it in an interview with *People*, "I don't feel like I'm gay. I just feel like I'm in love."

DeGeneres had hoped that by coming out and going public with her relationship with Heche, attention from the media—which, in the previous months, had grown so onerous she'd been forced to move from her home in Laurel Canyon to one in the more private and secure Beverly Hills—would subside. Instead, it grew. DeGeneres began to understand that the fame she had so longed for came with a price. It was, she said, like living in a fishbowl. And, she noted, "The more famous you get, the more people tap on the bowl." But, she acknowledged, "They are the same people who feed you."

CHAPTER FOUR

Ellen's Return

I n the spring of 1997, Ellen DeGeneres was on top of the world. She was in love. She had come out of the closet, and the character she played on her sitcom, *Ellen*, had done the same. And network executives had renewed her show for a fifth season.

But the media scrutiny, which had reached a fever pitch when DeGeneres came out, did not **abate**—and the coverage had taken a nasty turn. "Everybody got so sick of it," she said, "it got to the point that even Elton John, who I had never met in my life … said, 'We know you're gay. Shut up and be funny.'" She added, "You can imagine how much that hurt me."

DeGeneres's sitcom *Ellen* ran from 1994 to 1998.

Crises

By the fall, life had become increasingly grim. *Ellen* finished the season rated a disappointing twenty-third. On October 10, *Variety*, which covers the movie industry, reported a rift between DeGeneres, the network, her **distributor**, and her producers. The magazine reported that this tension was caused by disagreements as to what direction the show would take following the famous coming-out episode. Adding fuel to the fire was the fact that ABC placed a parental advisory on an episode in which DeGeneres and actress Joely Fisher shared a light-hearted kiss. *Variety* described DeGeneres as furious.

What was the problem? As noted in *Time*, "Instead of being integrated into the show, Ellen's homosexuality has become the show. *Ellen* is now as one-dimensional as *Bewitched*, where every storyline, every moment, every gag relies on the same device." The show just wasn't… *funny*. When the show began to rely on DeGeneres's sexuality above all else, the characters' humor fell flat.

"I tried to incorporate educational things about what people actually go through when they're coming out," DeGeneres later told the *New York Times Magazine*. "And it wasn't funny. Because it's not funny." Finally, in April 1998, the network cancelled the show.

It's likely DeGeneres was relieved by the network's decision. After all, she was slated to appear in a Ron Howard film, *EDtv*, alongside Jenna Elfman, Woody

Harrelson, and Matthew McConaughey. She had also signed on for *The Love Letter*, with Kate Capshaw and Blythe Danner. (Both films would be met with mixed reviews.) But then … nothing. DeGeneres's phone simply stopped ringing.

This was her greatest fear, DeGeneres told the *Los Angeles Times* in November 1998. "I lost my show. I've been attacked like hell. I went from making a lot of money on a sitcom to making no money." She was sure that her career was over. Heche found herself similarly blacklisted.

In late 1998, DeGeneres and Heche fired their agents and publicist and moved to Ojai, California, in an effort to escape the media glare. Then the couple caught a break: The release of *Six Days, Seven Nights*, in which Heche starred with Harrison Ford—she had inked the deal before going public with DeGeneres—resuscitated her career. In June 1999, DeGeneres and Heche moved back to Los Angeles.

A year later, in August 2000, Heche left DeGeneres. The split took everyone—including DeGeneres— by surprise.

"It was the first time I ever had my heart broken," DeGeneres admitted to the *Los Angeles Times*. "I'd always been the one to leave the relationship." She told *W* magazine, "When Anne left, I'd wake up in the morning, and my eyes would just immediately fill up with tears, and I would start convulsively crying."

Eventually, though, DeGeneres pieced her heart back together. How? "I finally just thought," she said, "I'm not going to let this destroy me." Soon, things would start to look up again.

A Fish Called Ellen

In 2001, DeGeneres's career began to pick up steam. That year, she returned to prime-time TV with a new sitcom, *The Ellen Show*. But unfortunately, in spite of the show's stellar cast—it featured such comedy legends as Martin Mull and Cloris Leachman, as well as the up-and-coming comic Jim Gaffigan—it was canceled after just three months.

"I lost my show, and I lost my entire career, and I lost everything for three years," DeGeneres said. And then … a lifeline. DeGeneres was offered the role of Dory, an amnesiac blue tang fish, in the animated film *Finding Nemo*, produced by Pixar. In fact, as she explained, the film's writer, Andrew Stanton, "had heard my voice on TV and how I never stayed on topic, and he wrote Dory with me in mind."

The film, released in May 2003, was a hit for critics and audiences alike. It was nominated for three Academy Awards and won one—the Academy Award for Best Animated Feature. It was the second highest-grossing film of 2003 and became the best-selling DVD of all time. In 2008, it was named one of the top ten greatest animated films of all time by the American Film Institute.

Ellen DeGeneres was back—and bigger than ever!

Daytime TV Calls

In September of 2003, DeGeneres launched another TV show: *The Ellen DeGeneres Show*. Unlike her previous shows, which were prime-time sitcoms, *The Ellen DeGeneres Show* was a daytime talk show. "I want the show to reach people and to be something positive," DeGeneres said. "Because the world is full of a lot of fear and a lot of negativity and a lot of judgment. I just think people need to start shifting into joy and happiness. As corny as it sounds, we need to make a shift."

The Ellen DeGeneres Show was an immediate success. For its very first season, the show was nominated for an impressive eleven Daytime Emmy Awards. To DeGeneres's delight, it won four, including Best Talk Show. These would be just the first of many Daytime Emmys for DeGeneres—to date, she's won twenty-seven.

Clearly, DeGeneres had found her medium. "I love the show," she said in 2004. "I love doing it. I get so much from it." Indeed, she loves the show so much, and it's been so successful, that she still does it as of this writing—and plans to continue until at least 2020.

Producing a show like *The Ellen DeGeneres Show* is a lot of work. "Every single day, it is my stamp on

DeGeneres with cast members of *The Ellen Show*

everything—it's my name—so I have to answer every question. I have to make every decision," DeGeneres said. "I have an amazing team, I have amazing producers, I have amazing writers, but at the end of it, it's me making the decisions on the writing, the tone, the editing."

DeGeneres embraced the challenge because she remembered what it felt to hit rock bottom—an experience she now calls "a blessing." In her typical tongue-in-cheek manner, she explains,

When I came out of the closet on my sitcom I knew it was a risk, but I took the risk and look what happened. It got canceled. Not the point. The point is, I got back on my horse … and I pushed forward. I said, 'You'll show them, Ellen!' And I did another sitcom. Guess what happened? That got canceled, too. Not the point, either. The real point is that I kept going, and now I appreciate my success more than I could have ever imagined.

Model Citizen

Thanks to the success of *The Ellen DeGeneres Show*, DeGeneres became a spokesperson for many companies, including American Express, J. C. Penney, and, perhaps most notably, CoverGirl Cosmetics.

To some, DeGeneres seemed an unlikely choice for CoverGirl. A CoverGirl representative explained the company's choice by calling her "an authentic beauty," noting that DeGeneres appealed to consumers "looking not so much for a role model as a woman they can relate to both physically and emotionally. In Ellen, she sees a slightly better version of herself, someone appealing from the inside out." According to an industry insider, DeGeneres was appealing for another reason: her rise, fall, and resurrection. "The idea of reinventing yourself is huge," the insider said. "Second-act stories give [middle-aged women] inspiration and strength."

CoverGirl Ellen DeGeneres

DeGeneres, joked, "I remember after I became a CoverGirl, people started labeling me as just another 'gorgeous blond model with a pretty face.'" Still, in her book *Seriously ... I'm Kidding*, DeGeneres reassured her fans that she understood what true beauty was. "True beauty is not related to what color your hair is or what color your eyes are," she wrote. "True beauty is about who you are as a human being, your principles, your moral compass."

Ellen Meets Her "Perfect Fit"

Having been burned by Anne Heche, DeGeneres was hesitant to date again. But in 2000, mutual friends introduced her to actress/director/photographer Alexandra Hedison. They started dating in 2001.

DeGeneres gushed about Hedison, describing her as incredibly kind and a source of happiness in her life. The pair split in 2004, however, after DeGeneres reconnected with Portia de Rossi, then thirty-one, at an awards show. The pair had met three years before; this time, sparks flew. "Ellen and Portia seemed totally into each other," a witness to their meeting reported. "Their body language was intense."

De Rossi, who hails from Australia, was introduced to American viewers during her tenure as lawyer Nelle Porter on *Ally McBeal*, which aired from 1997 to 2002. Starting in 2003, she starred in the popular show *Arrested Development*. But initially, de Rossi was perhaps best known for her very public struggles with **anorexia** and **bulimia**. By 2000, the actress, who stands five feet eight inches tall, weighed a skeletal eighty-two pounds—a number she achieved by eating just three hundred calories a day and taking handfuls of laxatives. Although she tried to hide her eating disorder, it was clear to everyone with eyes that she was ill.

It wasn't just her eating disorder that de Rossi sought to keep secret. She also hid her sexuality. Although she had known from a young age that she was gay, it was hard for de Rossi to imagine living openly as a gay woman. "My struggle with anorexia, coming to terms with my sexuality, I realized I had struggled with self-acceptance my whole life," she said.

It was DeGeneres who helped de Rossi—whose weight had doubled by 2004 due to her eating issues—gain self-acceptance. Although de Rossi felt terribly overweight,

Who Is Portia de Rossi?

Portia de Rossi was born on January 31, 1973, to parents Barry and Margaret Rogers in Australia. Her given name is Amanda Lee Rogers.

When Amanda was just nine years old, her father died, leaving Margaret to care for Amanda and her brother. To help make ends meet, Amanda began modeling for print and TV commercials. At 15, she changed her name to Portia de Rossi. The name Portia came from the heroine in Shakespeare's play *The Merchant of Venice.* As for de Rossi, she simply felt it sounded more exotic than Rogers.

After high school, de Rossi enrolled at the University of Melbourne, where she studied law. Although she was a diligent student, she could not resist the call of acting. In 1993, she auditioned for and was cast in the low-budget comedy *Sirens*, starring Hugh Grant and Elle McPherson. The next year, she moved to Los Angeles, intent on making it as an actress.

In 1996, de Rossi married documentary filmmaker Met Metcalfe for a **green card**. However, she said, she couldn't go through with getting the green card. After that, she dated a woman, Francesca Gregorini, stepdaughter of Ringo Starr. "I had a great relationship with Francesca," de Rossi recalled. "But I just kind of knew deep down in my heart that there was the possibility of something more."

In 2004, de Rossi found that "something more" ... with DeGeneres.

DeGeneres with Australian actress (and future wife) Portia de Rossi

DeGeneres didn't mind. "The fact that she noticed me at that point, and liked who I was, was kind of significant," de Rossi said later. She continued, "She seems to like the person that I really am. So that kind of gave me the courage to think that maybe other people will, too. And that includes being gay and being very open about it and having had some struggles in the past."

"I could say the same thing I've said in every relationship: 'I'm happy,'" DeGeneres told People in 2007. "But there's happiness and there's love, and then there's completion." She continued, "It doesn't take away from any of the relationships that I've had, [because] I've had amazing relationships ... But I feel like I found my perfect fit."

CHAPTER FIVE

Ellen the Activist

I'm not an **activist**," Ellen DeGeneres has said. Nevertheless, when she came out, DeGeneres quickly found herself associated with the hot-button issue of gay rights. As noted by author Kathleen Tracy, "Ellen became a symbol, whether she chose to or not, of gays' now insistent quest for, if not mass public blessing, then at the very least tolerance and respect." Eventually, DeGeneres would embrace this fact. While DeGeneres was dating Anne Heche, the pair met with President Clinton three times to discuss gay rights. DeGeneres also spoke at a rally in support of the Hate Crimes Prevention Act and appeared at the Equality Rocks Concert in Washington, DC.

Ellen DeGeneres is known not only for her comedy, but for her gay rights activism.

Gay Rights

DeGeneres wasn't just concerned about gay rights for her own sake. It was for the sake of all gay people. After the coming-out episode on *Ellen*, she began receiving letters from people who were discriminated against due to their sexuality. This greatly affected DeGeneres, who was shocked by the horrible experiences many gay people have endured.

"I remember the first letter I got, where somebody said I saved their life," she told *ABC News*. "They were going to kill themselves and they didn't because of what I did." She was particularly moved by the plight of gay teenagers. "There were kids who were committing suicide and people being beaten up," she recalled.

For DeGeneres, the issue of gay marriage was especially important. "I would love to have the same rights as everybody else," DeGeneres has said. "I don't care if it's called marriage. I don't care if it's called … domestic partnership. I don't care what it's called." For DeGeneres, like so many other gay people, being married wasn't merely symbolic. There were practical reasons for wanting to be married. Some gay couples were together for many years, but didn't have the rights married couples had, including not being allowed to visit one another in the hospital if one of them is sick, and not having certain tax benefits. If one of them died, she said, "they lose their house … the taxes kill them … because they're not married."

DeGeneres wasn't the only member of her family who was a vocal supporter of gay rights. Her mother, Betty, had also become an activist for the cause. Betty DeGeneres always accepted her daughter's sexuality, but it was only when her daughter publicly came out that she became a spokeswoman for gay rights and wrote a book about her path to activism. "Why feel so threatened by it?" she has said. "People who are in loving relationships that go on for twenty-five [or] thirty years have no recourse if one of them is deathly ill in the hospital." She added, "You know, if the world doesn't want to call it marriage, then let them call it a legal commitment. But it should happen."

In May 2008, the California Supreme Court struck down a law banning gay marriage. DeGeneres was overjoyed. She and de Rossi had wanted to marry for some time, and on August 16 that same year, they did just that. The event was intimate—just nineteen people attended the ceremony, held at DeGeneres and de Rossi's Los Angeles home—but lavish, with de Rossi wearing a gown by Zac Posen and DeGeneres clad in a matching suit.

Shortly after DeGeneres and de Rossi's wedding, Californians were asked to vote on a controversial bill called **Proposition 8**, which would prohibit same-sex marriage. On her blog, DeGeneres spoke out against the bill. "There's a California Proposition on the ballot that's a little confusing," she wrote. "It's called, 'The California

DeGeneres and de Rossi tie the knot.

Marriage Protection Act'—but don't let the name
fool you." She continued, "It's not protecting anyone's
marriage. Not yours. Not mine." And anyway, DeGeneres
joked in her typical fashion, "I can't return the wedding
gifts. I love my new toaster."

To DeGeneres and de Rossi's dismay, Proposition 8 passed. "This morning, when it was clear that Proposition 8 had passed in California, I can't explain the feeling I had," DeGeneres wrote in a statement. "I was saddened beyond belief." She continued, "I believe one day a 'ban on gay marriage' will sound totally ridiculous. In the meantime, I will continue to speak out for equality for all of us."

At first, DeGeneres and de Rossi worried that the passage of Proposition 8 nullified their marriage. Fortunately, a subsequent decision by the California Supreme Court ruled that their marriage was lawful because it occurred before Proposition 8 passed. Of their marriage, de Rossi—who, in 2009, would take DeGeneres's last name—remarked, "It's legal, and it's real, so there's a kind of formality to it that makes it very valid." Still, she felt for other gay and lesbian couples who were denied the right to legally marry. "Every day of our lives is a protest against the passing of Prop 8," de Rossi declared, calling the passage of the Proposition "devastating."

In 2010, a federal court ruled that Proposition 8 was **"unconstitutional** ... because no compelling state interest justifies denying same-sex couples the fundamental right to marry." The law also violated the Equal Protection Clause because "there is no rational basis for limiting the designation of 'marriage' to opposite-sex couples." But the federal court issued a **stay** on the ruling, meaning same-sex couples would continue to be denied the right to marry pending appeal.

The Ninth Circuit Court of Appeals upheld the ruling of the lower federal court, concluding that it is "implausible to think that denying two men or two women the right to call themselves married could somehow bolster the stability of families headed by one man and one woman." But the stay remained in place. Gay couples still could not be married in California, pending the case's review by the US Supreme Court. Before the review occurred, however, the US Supreme Court ruled on another gay-rights case, overturning the **Defense of Marriage Act (DOMA),** which denied federal benefits to same-sex couples. This ruling, which occurred on June 26, 2013, prompted the Ninth Circuit Court of Appeals to lift the stay preventing gay couples from being married. At last, gay couples in California—indeed, all across the nation—were able to wed. "It's a supremely wonderful day for equality," DeGeneres tweeted. "Prop 8 is over, and so is DOMA. Congratulations, everyone. And I mean everyone."

Humanitarian Causes

Of course, DeGeneres cares about *all* people—which explains her tireless efforts to bring awareness to several issues that affect humankind. One of these is AIDS awareness. Her activism in this area prompted then–

What About Kids?

For years, the press has harangued DeGeneres about whether she wanted to have children. And for years, the answer has been no. "Even before I knew I was gay, I knew I didn't want to have a child," DeGeneres told Stone Phillips in 2004. "Listen, I love babies. I love children. And I melt when I'm around them." But, she added, "I also love my freedom, and I love that I can sleep at night."

Fortunately, de Rossi agreed. "You have to really want to have kids, and neither of us did," she told *Out* magazine in 2013. "So it's just going to be me and Ellen and no babies." But, she said, "we're the best of friends, and married life is blissful, it really is."

Secretary of State Hillary Clinton to name DeGeneres a Special **Envoy** for Global AIDS Awareness. Needless to say, DeGeneres was honored by the appointment, noting that "[t]he fight against AIDS is something that has always been close to my heart. And I'm happy that I can use my platform to educate people and spread hope." She added, with her usual self-deprecating humor, "Now, if you'll excuse me, I have to go look up what 'envoy' means."

DeGeneres often donates money to causes that relate to her own upbringing and experiences. For example, to help her former neighbors in the city of New Orleans

DeGeneres is a passionate supporter of animal rights.

rebuild after Hurricane Katrina in 2005, DeGeneres lent her support to the American Red Cross's Hurricane Katrina Relief Fund. She also supported Make It Right, a charity set up by actor Brad Pitt that is dedicated to building new homes for those affected by the disaster. And, in honor of her mother, who survived breast cancer,

DeGeneres has teamed up with Susan G. Komen for the Cure to raise awareness for breast cancer. During her "Ellen for the Cure" campaign, run each October in commemoration of Breast Cancer Awareness Month, DeGeneres uses her show to give out prizes and raise donations for the cause.

Animal Rights

DeGeneres doesn't just care about rights for people. She's also a passionate crusader for animal rights. "I have always loved animals," DeGeneres wrote in her book *My Point … And I Do Have One*. "When I was about eleven years old, I wanted to be a veterinarian." She explained, "I think I realized, even at an early age, that the real beauty of pets is that they love you unconditionally. All they would like in return is a bit of attention and some food." She added, "And, the food doesn't even have to be that good. It could just come out of a can." Perhaps this explains why DeGeneres and de Rossi have three cats and three dogs—all rescues—and why she became part owner of Halo Purely for Pets, which makes healthy dog food.

Although DeGeneres was raised eating meat dishes like steak, she eventually went **vegan**. DeGeneres convinced de Rossi to go vegan as well. To encourage others to make the leap, DeGeneres features a "Going Vegan with DeGeneres" page on the website for her talk show, promoting "Meatless Mondays" and sharing vegan recipes.

DeGeneres and de Rossi visit the Taronga Zoo in Sydney, Australia.

DeGeneres has used her platform as a person in the public eye to raise awareness for animal rights—and she's not afraid to put her money where her mouth is. In 2013, she donated twenty-five thousand dollars to support efforts to stop an **ag-gag law**. (An ag-gag law is one that "forbid[s] the act of undercover filming of photography of activity on farms without the consent of their owner"—a practice that makes it easier for operators to hide the abuse of the animals in their care.)

DeGeneres serves as an ambassador for Farm Sanctuary, an organization that shelters and works on behalf of abused farm animals, and supports The Gentle Barn, which houses and provides veterinary care for more than 170 rescued animals. She also works closely with The Humane Society to share information with her viewers about animals and animal rights. DeGeneres's support of animal rights prompted People for the Ethical Treatment of Animals (PETA) to name her "Woman of the Year" in 2009.

For DeGeneres, the matter of animal rights is part of the larger issue of caring for our planet. She writes:

> *The more we consciously think about what we're doing and what we're consuming, the better off we're going to be. And I don't just mean what we eat. I mean what we buy and what we use. We consume so much. We buy the latest computers and phones and TVs and clothing, and that means everything that came before it ends up in landfills and oceans. I know that's not a particularly hilarious sentiment but it's something we need to think about as humans.*

Ellen's *Real* Legacy

Clearly, Ellen DeGeneres is passionate about a great many causes. But perhaps the one that is dearest to her is simply spreading happiness. "My whole career has been based on making people feel happy. That's all I ever wanted to do—was make people laugh and make people happy," she has said.

For DeGeneres, a key aspect to happiness is self-acceptance. In her book *Seriously ... I'm Kidding*, she

Ellen the Philanthropist

There's no denying it: Ellen DeGeneres is serious about philanthropy. According to the website Look to the Stars: The World of Celebrity Giving, DeGeneres has supported some forty-five charities and foundations and thirty different causes. Not surprisingly, some pertain to gay rights (GLAAD, GLSEN, It Gets Better Project, and The Trevor Project), and others are to promote animal rights (American Wild Horse Preservation Campaign, Best Friends Animal Society, Farm Sanctuary, Halo Pet Foundation, PETA, Society for Animal Protective Legislation, The Gentle Barn, and The Humane Society). But DeGeneres also gives to various other causes, including education (Andre Agassi Foundation for Education and Save the Music Foundation), the fight against racism (Artists Against Racism), hunger (Feeding America), homelessness (Habitat for Humanity), and bullying (STOMP Out Bullying).

wrote, "Accept who you are." Then, to cover her bases, she added, "Unless you're a serial killer." DeGeneres urged her readers to listen to themselves first and be strong enough to stand up for their own beliefs, even though others may disagree with them: "Find out who you are and figure out what you believe in. Even if it's different from what your neighbors believe in and different from what your parents believe in. Stay true to yourself. Have your own opinion. Don't worry about what people say about you or think about you."

Perhaps most importantly, as she told the graduating class at Tulane University in 2009, "Follow your passion. Stay true to yourself." She then quipped, "Never follow someone else's path unless you're in the woods and you're lost and you see a path. By all means, you should follow that."

Besides, as DeGeneres wrote in *Seriously . . . I'm Kidding*,

I personally like being unique. I like being my own person with my own style and my own opinions and my own toothbrush. I think it's so much better to stand out in some way and to set yourself apart from the masses. It would be so boring to look out into the world and see hundreds of people who look and think exactly like me." She adds, "If I wanted that, I could just sit in front of a mirror and admire my own reflection all day. That's already how I spend my mornings. I don't need to spend all of my time doing that.

DeGeneres understands that she's a role model—particularly for girls and women—and she takes it to heart. She has mentioned that she, too, had strong female role models as she set forth in her career, including

Lucille Ball, Carol Burnett, Barbara Walters, Diane Sawyer, and Oprah Winfrey. These women "paved the way" for DeGeneres's own success. She writes:

And now that I have my own show on television I feel a sense of responsibility to follow in their footsteps and have a positive influence on the young girls and women who watch me every day. That's why I keep things light and upbeat and it's why I try to have powerful and influential women on my show to serve as examples for the people at home. I love having women like Michelle Obama and Hillary Clinton on my show. I also love having regular, everyday women on my show with inspiring stories about their personal journey.

DeGeneres with Secretary of State Hillary Clinton on *The Ellen DeGeneres Show*

Summing up, DeGeneres writes, "Anyway, I just want to be able to use the platform I have in front of millions of people around the world every day for good things. I want young girls to know that they should dream big and that if they put their minds to it they can accomplish anything."

Still, DeGeneres longs for a world where gender is no longer relevant. "Maybe at some point we won't have to break success down along gender lines," she writes in *Seriously … I'm Kidding.* "Maybe we won't have to say a man did this or a woman invented that. Maybe we'll just be able to say that this wonderful, smart, creative person did something extraordinary and that will be that."

CHAPTER SIX

Ellen Expands

During the course of her thirty-plus year career, Ellen DeGeneres has won countless awards. These include one Primetime Emmy for Outstanding Writing for a Comedy Series ("The Puppy Episode," *Ellen*, 1996) and three American Comedy Awards—two for Funniest Female Performer in a TV Special (1995 and 2001) and one for Funniest Female Standup Comic (1991). DeGeneres has also won fifteen People's Choice Awards, including five for Favorite Daytime TV Host (2005–2006, 2012, 2014–2015), four for Favorite Funny Female Star (2005–2008), and three for Favorite Talk Show Host (2007–2009). Perhaps most impressive are DeGeneres's twenty-seven Daytime

A joyful Ellen DeGeneres holds onto two of her many Emmy awards.

Emmy Awards, including nine for Outstanding Talk Show (2004–2007, 2010–2011, 2013–2015) and four for Outstanding Talk Show Host (2005–2008). And, in 2012, DeGeneres earned what all celebrities long for: a star on the Walk of Fame in Hollywood.

Receiving—and Giving—Recognition

But for Ellen DeGeneres, it is better to give than to receive—and that goes for recognition, too. For this reason, DeGeneres has become a regular host of various awards programs. Her first was the 46th Primetime Emmy Awards, in 1994, which she co-hosted with actress Patricia Richardson. In 1996 and 1997, she presided over the Grammy Awards.

In 2001, DeGeneres was given another opportunity to host the Primetime Emmys. Originally scheduled for September 16, the show was postponed due to the 9/11 attacks, which occurred five days prior. When, seven weeks later, the show aired, DeGeneres brought some much-needed laughter to the live audience and the American public. Her most memorable line: "I felt it was important for me to be here tonight, because what would bug the Taliban more than seeing a gay woman in a suit surrounded by Jews?" As noted by *Today* contributor Randee Dawn, "The joke landed and secured her as warm, funny, identifiable—and able to deliver a careful barb." DeGeneres's deft performance earned her a standing ovation at the end of the show.

DeGeneres would again host the Primetime Emmy Awards in the wake of a national tragedy, this time in 2005, just weeks after Hurricane Katrina devastated her hometown of New Orleans and much of the Gulf Coast. This was a more somber affair, made even more poignant for DeGeneres by its tribute to her idol, the great Johnny Carson, who had died earlier that year. Still, DeGeneres managed to elicit a few laughs. "This is the second time I've hosted the Emmy's after a national tragedy, and I just want to say that I'm honored, because it's times like this that we really, really need laughter," DeGeneres began. Then she quipped, "And be sure to look for me next month when I host the North Korean People's Choice Awards."

It was a natural progression for DeGeneres to host the Academy Awards, also called the Oscars, which she did in 2007. It was not without trepidation, however. A great many stars had served as host, with many failing to deliver an entertaining Oscar broadcast. Indeed, "There is no more challenging hosting job in show business," noted producer Laura Ziskin. "It requires someone who can keep the show alive and fresh and moving, as well as someone who is a flat-out great entertainer." But DeGeneres received rave reviews. "The only complaint," observed legendary TV host Regis Philbin of the broadcast, "was there's not enough DeGeneres."

DeGeneres slayed the Academy Awards audience with lines like this one: "What a wonderful night, such diversity in the room, in a year when there's been so many negative things said about people's race, religion, and sexual orientation." She continued, "And I want to put this out there: If there weren't blacks, Jews and gays, there would be no Oscars, or anyone named Oscar, when you think about that." Indeed, her performance was so solid, it earned her a Primetime Emmy nomination.

The Academy of Motion Picture Arts and Sciences, which organizes the Academy Awards, tapped DeGeneres to host the Oscars for a second time, in 2014. Even though, as DeGeneres said, "Hosting the Oscars

This selfie taken by DeGeneres during the 2014 Academy Award, featuring several A-list actors, became the most retweeted image ever.

is pretty much the scariest thing you can do," likening it to bungee jumping, she agreed to take on the task. "I'm comfortable right now," she explained. "And it's never good to be comfortable as a performer."

Once again, the broadcast was a success. DeGeneres delighted the live audience by ordering pizza for the first several rows, using musician Pharrell's hat to collect the money needed to pay the deliveryman. And she set the record for the most retweeted image ever, assembling several A-list actors—including Jared Leto, Jennifer Lawrence, Channing Tatum, Meryl Streep, Julia Roberts, Kevin Spacey, Brad Pitt, Lupita Nyong'O, Angelina Jolie, and Bradley Cooper—for a group selfie. "Best photo ever," read the caption.

Finding Dory

Speaking of The Academy Awards, in 2003, a movie in which DeGeneres starred, *Finding Nemo*, won the Oscar for Best Animated Picture. In the years that followed, DeGeneres regularly lobbied for a chance to reprise her role as Dory, the forgetful blue tang fish.

In her book *Seriously … I'm Kidding*, DeGeneres included a comical series of "journal entries." The series started with an entry from May 30, 2003. "Remember that movie *Finding Nemo?*" DeGeneres wrote. "Well it came out today and guess what—it set the record for best opening day ever of an animated movie!" She continued, "I wouldn't be surprised if Pixar called me today to say they want to make a sequel." The "journal's" next entry, dated August 1, 2003, noted, "*Finding Nemo* is now the highest-grossing animated movie of all time! Can you believe it?! Hang on, my phone's ringing. It's probably Pixar telling me they want to make a sequel." In the next day's entry, DeGeneres wrote, "That phone call wasn't about *Finding Nemo 2*, but I'm sure they'll call any minute." Fast-forward nearly eight years to an entry from June 24, 2011: "You know what comes out today, Journal? *Cars 2*. Isn't that great? A sequel to a hit animated movie. I'm so, so, so happy for them."

Her "journal" wasn't the only place in which DeGeneres expressed her desire to make a follow-up to *Finding Nemo*. She also repeatedly lobbied for a sequel on her daytime talk show, *The Ellen DeGeneres Show*. Why was she so keen to reprise the role of Dory? One obvious reason was the likelihood of a significant paycheck. But DeGeneres had another reason:

> [Dory] is a really sweet character. And she's flawed, and I think it's important for kids to grow up and see flawed characters that are lovable. No matter if they make mistake after mistake, they have a little surrounding pack. Even though they're frustrated with her they love her.

No doubt, DeGeneres identified with Dory— particularly Dory's wise catchphrase, "Just keep swimming." "'Just keep swimming' certainly applies to me and to a lot of people out there," DeGeneres said.

Finally, DeGeneres's constant badgering paid off. In 2013, Pixar, the studio behind *Finding Nemo*, announced that it would produce a sequel, called *Finding Dory*. "I have waited for this day for a long, long, long, long, long, long time," said DeGeneres in a statement. She added, tongue in cheek, "I'm not mad it took this long. I know the people at Pixar were busy creating *Toy Story 16*." On her talk show, DeGeneres played a montage of her on-air pleas for a sequel before sharing the news. "Kids, let that be a lesson to you," she added. "Anything is possible if you're patient and beg enough on national television."

What would *Finding Dory* be about? Director Andrew Stanton explained, "One thing we couldn't stop thinking about was why [Dory] was all alone in the ocean on the day she met [Nemo's dad] Marlin." He continued, "In *Finding Dory*, she will be reunited with her loved ones, learning a few things about the meaning of family along the way."

"The script is fantastic," DeGeneres gushed. "It has everything I loved about the first one: It's got a lot of heart, it's really funny, and the best part is—it's got a lot more Dory."

Fans of *Finding Nemo* will recognize several of the same voices in *Finding Dory*, including Albert Brooks as Marlin, Nemo's father; Willem Dafoe as Gill; and Vicki Lewis as Deb. (The voice of Nemo is played by a new actor, Hayden Rolence; the actor who played Nemo in 2003 has long since grown up, and his voice has changed accordingly.) In addition, *Finding Dory* includes such stars as Diane Keaton and Eugene Levy (Dory's parents), Ed O'Neill (Hank the octopus), and Ty Burrell (Bailey the beluga whale). Idris Elba and Dominic West also star. As of this writing, the film has not yet been released, but it is due in theaters in June 2016.

A Very Good Production

In 2003, DeGeneres launched her own production company, called A Very Good Production. This company has produced *The Ellen DeGeneres Show* from the outset. A Very Good Production has also had a hand in many other projects—and there are more in the works.

One project is an animated TV series based on the famous book *Green Eggs and Ham* by Dr. Seuss, which will air starting in 2018 via streaming on Netflix. "It's going to be cutting-edge animation," DeGeneres said of the show. "It's never been done on television before. It's very, very cool. I'm excited about it." In addition to *Green Eggs and Ham*, DeGeneres's production company bought the rights to another popular children's book: *Castle Hangnail* by Ursula Vernon. Rather than a TV show, *Castle Hangnail*, a fantasy book, will be a feature-length film. Rights to a third book, a young adult fantasy novel called *Uprooted*, have also been secured.

DeGeneres's production company doesn't just produce projects geared toward children, however. One sitcom in development features Idina Menzel, perhaps best known for voicing the role of Princess Elsa in the animated hit *Frozen*. Tentatively called *Happy Time*, the show centers around a woman who lives in the public eye and wants to stop pretending she is always happy. Another TV project geared toward adults is an adaptation of the book *Someday, Someday, Maybe* by Lauren Graham, an actress who has starred in *Gilmore Girls* and *Parenthood*.

No doubt, Ellen DeGeneres will continue to produce projects about which she is passionate for many years to come!

Ellen DeGeneres: Lifestyle Guru

In recent years, Ellen DeGeneres has expanded her empire beyond entertainment. These days, she's also a lifestyle guru. In 2014, she launched a line of home products, branded E.D., on the home shopping network QVC. "I am thrilled to launch my home line on QVC," DeGeneres said of the venture. "I wouldn't do it with anyone else because QVC combines everything I love: shopping, watching TV, and acronyms."

The line features items with DeGeneres's distinct style. DeGeneres has always been interested in interior design. In fact, she has such a good eye for design that her homes have appeared in such publications the *New York Times*, *Elle Décor*, and *Architectural Digest*.

In 2015, DeGeneres extended the E.D. brand to include clothing and accessories, offering them for sale through Bergdorf Goodman and through her own e-commerce site. "I have a very distinct way of dressing, and clearly other people are responding to it," she explained. "So that was the impetus to launch the brand."

Ellen DeGeneres with Chris Burch, her partner at E.D., at Bergdorf Goodman.

The clothing line, she said, "is not extremely feminine, it's not masculine, it's just comfortable."

DeGeneres's interest in style and design also led her to host a show on the HGTV network starting in 2014.

American Idol

In 2009, *American Idol*, the popular singing contest, tapped Ellen DeGeneres to serve as a judge for the ninth season, replacing Paula Abdul.

Why DeGeneres? Unlike the other judges on the panel—Simon Cowell, Randy Jackson, and Kara DioGuardi—DeGeneres was not part of the music industry. Simon Fuller, who created the show, explained it like this: "DeGeneres has been a fan of the show for many years, and her love of music and understanding of the American public will bring a unique human touch to our judging panel."

"Hopefully, I'm the people's point of view," DeGeneres said at the time. "I'm looking at it as a person who is going to buy the music and is going to relate to that person."

DeGeneres quickly realized she had made a mistake. For one thing, she had continued to appear in *The Ellen DeGeneres* show. Adding *Idol* to the mix meant she was burning the candle from both ends. More importantly, DeGeneres hated criticizing the contestants. "While I love discovering, supporting and nurturing young talent, it was hard for me to judge people and sometimes hurt their feelings," she explained. The show, DeGeneres said, "didn't feel like the right fit for me."

TALCOTT LIBRARY

Called *Ellen's Design Challenge*, the show challenges six furniture designers to sketch, design, and build furniture in a twenty-four-hour time period. Thanks to the show's success, it was picked up for a second season, in 2015.

Finally, DeGeneres shared her love of interior design in a new book, called *Home*. Featuring resplendent photos of several homes that DeGeneres has purchased and renovated during the past twenty-five years—including a glimpse of the Santa Barbara villa she now shares with de Rossi—the book shares various design principles that she has picked up along the way.

What's Next for Ellen?

Reflecting on her career, Ellen DeGeneres has mentioned the role that hard work has played in her success. In an interview with *W* magazine, she said:

> If I had ever thought that my career would have reached what it did before it dropped, much less then come back … I'm truly in an amazing, amazing place in my life. But I don't want to say I'm surprised, because at the same time, I created it, I thought it, I wanted this. So when I look back on it, every single thing I'm doing is what I've wanted, and I believe that you get what you want.

So what, then, did DeGeneres "get"? She became the "Funniest Person in America." She was called to the couch by Johnny Carson. She starred in her own sitcom, for which she won a Primetime Emmy. She starred in an Oscar-winning animated film. She hosts the top daytime TV program, for which she has nabbed more than two dozen Daytime Emmys. She has an enormous social media following, boasting nearly fifty-three million Twitter followers and more than twenty-three million Facebook fans. In 2015, *Forbes* magazine named DeGeneres the fiftieth most powerful woman in the world, with an estimated net worth of seventy-five million dollars. And of course, she changed the national conversation about gay people and gay rights.

What's next for Ellen DeGeneres? What more could she reasonably want to achieve?

We know she'll continue with *The Ellen DeGeneres Show* until at least 2020. She'll likely develop more projects with her production company. And she'll work on growing her E.D. clothing, accessories, and home goods brand.

Beyond that, the sky's the limit.

Timeline

1986

DeGeneres performs on *The Tonight Show with Johnny Carson* on November 28 and is the first female comic invited by Johnny to sit on his couch and chat after her set.

1972

Elliott and Betty DeGeneres divorce.

Ellen Lee DeGeneres is born to Elliott and Betty DeGeneres on January 26.

1958

DeGeneres is voted "Funniest Person in America.

1982

DeGeneres performs a stand-up routine for the first time.

1980

1998

Ellen is cancelled in April. This is the start of a difficult few years for DeGeneres.

2013

The US Supreme Court clears the way for same-sex marriage once and for all on June 26.

1994

The first episode of *These Friends of Mine*, a sitcom developed around DeGeneres and later called simply *Ellen*, airs on March 29.

2008

DeGeneres marries longtime love Portia de Rossi on August 16, just months before Californians vote to make same-sex marriage illegal.

"The Puppy Episode," in which DeGeneres's character on *Ellen*, Ellen Morgan, comes out of the closet, airs on April 30. The same month, DeGeneres also comes out of the closet in real life.

1997

In May, DeGeneres makes her comeback as the voice of Dory in the Academy Award–winning animated film, *Finding Nemo*. That September, DeGeneres launches *The Ellen DeGeneres Show*, a daytime TV talk show that remains on the air as of this writing.

2003

SOURCE NOTES

Chapter One

Page 6: Tracy, Kathleen. *Ellen The Real Story of Ellen DeGeneres* (Secaucus, NJ: Carol Publishing Group, 1999) p.8.

Page 7: Tracy, *Ellen: The Real Story of Ellen DeGeneres*, p.6.

Page 7: DeGeneres, *My Point...And I Do Have One*, p.128.

Page 8: Tracy, *Ellen: The Real Story of Ellen DeGeneres*, p.9.

Page 8: Rabens, Chandler, "Ellen Uncensored," *Teen People*, February, 2006.

Page 8-9: Tracy, *Ellen: The Real Story of Ellen DeGeneres*, p.12.

Page 9: Tracy, *Ellen: The Real Story of Ellen DeGeneres*, p.13.

Page 12: Tracy, *Ellen: The Real Story of Ellen DeGeneres*, p.19.

Page 12: Silverman, Steven M., "Ellen DeGeneres Helped Mom with Cancer Fight," *People*, September 27, 2007, http://www.people.com/people/article/0,,20058779,00.html.

Page 13: Lehner, Marla, "Ellen DeGeneres: I Was Molested," *People*, May 18, 2005, www.people.com/people/article/0,,1062732,00.html.

Page 13: Hall, Sarah, "Ellen DeGeneres Talks Abuse," *E! Online*, May 18, 2005, www.eonline.com/news/49889/ellen-degeneres-talks-abuse.

Page 13: Tracy, *Ellen: The Real Story of Ellen DeGeneres*, p.28.

Page 14: Tracy, *Ellen: The Real Story of Ellen DeGeneres*, p.30.

Page 14: *Ibid.*

Page 15: Tracy, *Ellen: The Real Story of Ellen DeGeneres*, p.32.

Page 17: "Wry Toast," *People*, July 19, 1999, www.people.com/people/archive/article/0,,20128761,00.html.

Chapter Two

Page 20: Perkoff, *Another Lost Angel*, 2008.

Page 20: Capretto, Lisa, "How the Tragic Death of Ellen DeGeneres' Ex Changed Her Life," *Huffington Post*, October 26, 2015, www.huffingtonpost.com/entry/ellen-degeneres-ex-girlfriend-death_us.

Page 20: Foley, Bridget, "Ellen DeGeneres," *W*, March, 2007, www.wmagazine.com/people/celebrities/2007/03/ellen_degeneres.

Page 20: Capretto, "How the Tragic Death of Ellen DeGeneres' Ex Changed Her Life."

Page 22: DeGeneres, Ellen. *Phone Call to God*. Performed by Ellen DeGeneres. NBC TV West Coast Studios, Burbank, 1986.

Page 22-23: Tracy, *Ellen: The Real Story of Ellen DeGeneres*, p.38.

Page 23-24: Foley, "Ellen DeGeneres."

Page 24: Tracy, *Ellen: The Real Story of Ellen DeGeneres*, p.41.

Page 24: *Ibid.*

Page 25: Tracy, *Ellen The Real Story of Ellen DeGeneres*, p.47.

Page 26: DeGeneres, Ellen. *My Point...And I Do Have One* (New York: Bantam Books, 1995).

Page 27: Tracy, *Ellen: The Real Story of Ellen DeGeneres*, p.49.

Page 27: Tracy, *Ellen: The Real Story of Ellen DeGeneres*, p.52.

Page 27: Foley, "Ellen DeGeneres."

Page 28: Tracy, *Ellen: The Real Story of Ellen DeGeneres*, p.60.

Page 30: Foley, "Ellen DeGeneres."

Page 30: Rocca, Mo, "Ellen DeGeneres: My Job's to Make You Happy," *CBS News*, June 12, 2012, www.cbsnews.com/news/ellen-dege-neres-my-jobs-to-make-you-happy.

Page 31: Tracy, *Ellen: The Real Story of Ellen DeGeneres*, p.62.

Page 31: DeGeneres, *Phone Call to God*.

Page 31: *Ibid.*

Chapter Three

Page 34: Tracy, *Ellen: The Real Story of Ellen DeGeneres*, p.74.

Page 34: Tracy, *Ellen: The Real Story of Ellen DeGeneres*, p.75.

Page 35: Green, Jesse, "Come Out. Come Down. Come Back. Being Ellen DeGeneres," *New York Times Magazine*, August 19, 2001, www.nytimes.com/2001/08/19/magazine/come-out-come-down-come-back-being-ellen.html.

Page 35: Tracy, *Ellen: The Real Story of Ellen DeGeneres*, p.84.

Page 36: Tracy, *Ellen: The Real Story of Ellen DeGeneres*, p.110

Page 36–37: Tracy, *Ellen: The Real Story of Ellen DeGeneres*, p.108.

Page 37: Tracy, *Ellen: The Real Story of Ellen DeGeneres*, p.154.

pg 38: Tracy, *Ellen: The Real Story of Ellen DeGeneres*, p.132.

Page 39: Schwarzbaum, Lisa, *My Point...And I Do Have One, Entertain-ment Weekly*, September 8, 1995, www.ew.com/article/1995/09/08/book-review-my-point-and-i-do-have-one

Page 44: Tracy, *Ellen: The Real Story of Ellen DeGeneres*, p.221.

Page 44: Tracy, *Ellen: The Real Story of Ellen DeGeneres*, p.204.

Page 44: Tracy, *Ellen: The Real Story of Ellen DeGeneres*, p.205.

Page 45–46: Tracy, *Ellen: The Real Story of Ellen DeGeneres*, p.242.

Page 46: Tracy, *Ellen: The Real Story of Ellen DeGeneres*, p.124.

Page 46: Tracy, *Ellen: The Real Story of Ellen DeGeneres*, p.125.

Page 47: Tracy, *Ellen: The Real Story of Ellen DeGeneres*, p.184.

Page 47: Tracy, Ellen: *The Real Story of Ellen DeGeneres*, p.207.

Page 49: Tracy, *Ellen: The Real Story of Ellen DeGeneres*, p.227.

Page 49: Tracy, *Ellen: The Real Story of Ellen DeGeneres*, p.118.

Chapter Four

Page 51: Rothman, "Ellen DeGeneres Reveals the Negatives that Happened After Coming Out."

Page 52: Tracy, Ellen: *The Real Story of Ellen DeGeneres*, p.244.

Page 52: Green, "Come Out. Come Down. Come Back. Being Ellen DeGeneres."

Page 53: Tracy, Kathleen. *Ellen: The Real Story of Ellen DeGeneres*, p.255.

Page 53: Smolowe, Jill, "Yep, It's Over," *People*. September 4, 2004.

Page 54: Smolowe, "Yep, It's Over."

Page 54: Brownfield, Paul, "'The First Time I Ever Had My Heart Broken,'" *Los Angeles Times*, September 16, 2001.

Page 54: Foley, "Ellen DeGeneres."

Page 55: Chestang, Raphael, "EXCLUSIVE: Ellen DeGeneres Says 'Finding Nemo' Came Along at Her Lowest Point," *ET Online*, November 19, 2015, www.etonline.com/news/176466_exclusive_ellen_degeneres_says_finding_nemo_came_along_at_her_lowest_point.

Page 55: Chestang, "EXCLUSIVE: Ellen DeGeneres Says 'Finding Nemo' Came Along at Her Lowest Point."

Page 56: Foley, "Ellen DeGeneres."

Page 57: Phillips, Stone, "Catching Up with Ellen DeGeneres," *Dateline*, www.nbcnews.com/id/6430100/ns/dateline_nbc-newsmakers/t/catching-ellen-degeneres.

Page 57: Foley, "Ellen DeGeneres."

Page 57: DeGeneres, Ellen. *Seriously...I'm Kidding*. (New York, NY: Grand Central Publishing, 2001) p.30-31.

Page 58: La Ferla, Ruth, "Like the Makeup Model, Warts and All?" *New York Times*, September 19, 2008, www.nytimes.com/2008/09/21/fashion/21ellen.html.

Page 58: DeGeneres, *Seriously...I'm Kidding*, p.93

Page 59: DeGeneres, *Seriously...I'm Kidding*, p.5.

Page 59: Gardner, Chris, and Ulrica Wihlborg, "DeGeneres's New Squeeze: Portia de Rossi," *People*, December 15, 2004, www.people.com/people/article/0,,1007643,00.html.

Page 60: Nudd, Tim, "Ellen DeGeneres: Portia Is 'My Perfect Fit,'" *People*, January 27, 2007, www.people.com/people/article/0,,20009962,00.html.

Page 61: Jordan, Julie, "Chatting With...DeGeneres & Portia," *People*, September 1, 2008, www.people.com/people/archive/article/0,,20221816,00.html.

Page 61: Jordan, Julie, "Portia de Rossi: 'I Don't Want to Have Any More Secrets,'" *People*, November 3, 2010, www.people.com/people/article/0,,20438754,00.html.

Chapter Five

Page 63: Hochman, David, "Ellen DeGeneres: Nice Girls Finish First," *Good Housekeeping*, September 10, 2011, www.goodhousekeeping.com/life/inspirational-stories/interviews/a18893/ellen-degeneres-interview.

Page 63: Tracy, *Ellen: The Real Story of Ellen DeGeneres*, p.251.

Page 64: Rothman, "Ellen DeGeneres Reveals the Negatives that Happened After Coming Out," http://abcnews.go.com/Entertainment/ellen-degeneres-reveals-negatives-happened-coming/story?id=34764473.

Page 64: Green, "Come Out. Come Down. Come Back. Being Ellen DeGeneres," http://www.nytimes.com/2001/08/19/magazine/come-out-come-down-come-back-being-ellen.html.

Page 65: Phillips, "Catching up with Ellen DeGeneres."

Page 65–66: Tracy, *Ellen: The Real Story of Ellen DeGeneres*, p.239.

Page 67: Davis, Caris, "Ellen DeGeneres Defends the Right of Gay Marriage," *People*, September 24, 2008, www.people.com/people/article/0,,20228501,00.html.

Page 67: Silverman, "Ellen DeGeneres Reacts to Gay Marriage Ban," www.people.com/people/article/0,,20238579,00.html.

Page 67: Huver, Scott, "Portia de Rossi Is a Changed Woman Thanks to Marriage," *People*, January 17, 2008, www.people.com/people/article/0,,20253446,00.html.

Page 68: n.d. *California Proposition 8 (2008)*. Wikipedia.

Page 68: *Ibid.*

Page 69: "Ellen DeGeneres on DOMA & Prop 8 Rulings: 'It's a Supremely Wonderful Day,'" *People*, June 26, 2013, www.people.com/people/article/0,,20712433,00.html.

Page 69: Phillips, "Catching up with Ellen DeGeneres."

Page 69: Krochmal, S. N., "Portia de Rossi: That Girl!" *Out*, April 3, 2013, www.out.com/entertainment/television/2013/04/11/portia-de-rossi.

Page 71: "Ellen DeGeneres named global envoy for AIDS awareness," *Reuters*, November 9, 2011, http://www.reuters.com/article/us-ellendegeneres

Page 72: DeGeneres, *My Point...And I Do Have One*, p.151.

Page 73: n.d. *Ag-gag*. Wikipedia.

Page 73: DeGeneres, *Seriously...I'm Kidding*, p.160.

Page 75: Tracy, *Ellen: The Real Story of Ellen DeGeneres*, p.ix.

Page 75: DeGeneres, *Seriously...I'm Kidding*, p.240.

Page 75: "7 Amazing Graduation Commencement Speeches," Goodnet, May 23, 2013, www.goodnet.org/articles/7-amazing-graduation-commencement-speeches.

Page 77: DeGeneres, *Seriously...I'm Kidding*, p.56.

Page 77: DeGeneres, *Seriously...I'm Kidding*, p.178-179.

Chapter Six

Page 80: Dawn, Randee, "Ellen DeGeneres brings wit, charm back to Oscars hosting gig," *Today*, March 1, 2014, www.today.com/popculture/ellen-degeneres-brings-wit-charm-back-oscars-hosting-gig.

Page 80–81: Dawn, "Ellen DeGeneres brings wit, charm back to Oscars hosting gig."

Page 81: Gilman, Greg, "Ellen DeGeneres Returns as Oscar Host: 5 of Her Best Award Show Moments," *The Wrap*, August 3, 2013, www.thewrap.com/ellen-degeneres-returns-oscars-host-5-amazing-award-show-moments-video-108091.

Page 81: "Ellen DeGeneres to Host 79th Academy Awards Presentation," Academy of Motion Picture Arts and Sciences, September 7, 2006, www.oscars.org/press/pressreleases/2006/06.09.07.html.

Page 81: Smith, Michael, "Ellen DeGeneres the Delicious Irony of Hosting Oscar Ceremony Again," August 3, 2013, guardianlv.com/2013/08/DeGeneres-degeneres-the-delicious-irony-of-hosting-oscar-ceremony-again.

Page 82: Smith, "Ellen DeGeneres the Delicious Irony of Hosting Oscar Ceremony Again."

Page 83: DeGeneres and Leonard, "Ellen DeGeneres on Life, the Oscars and Finding True Love."

Page 83–84: DeGeneres, *Seriously...I'm Kidding*, p.35-41.

Page 84: Park, Andrea, "Just Keep Swimming! Ellen DeGeneres

Reveals the First Trailer for Nemo Sequel Finding Dory," *People*, November 10, 2015, www.people.com/article/finding-dory-ellen-degeneres-releases-first-trailer-nemo-sequel.

Page 84: Chestang, "EXCLUSIVE: Ellen DeGeneres Says 'Finding Nemo' Came Along at Her Lowest Point."

Page 85: Saad, Nardine, "Ellen DeGeneres rides tidal wave of excitement over 'Finding Dory,'" *Los Angeles Times*, April 3, 2015, articles.latimes.com/2013/apr/03/entertainment/la-et-mg-ellen-degeneres-finding-dory-20130403.

Page 85: *Ibid.*

Page 86: Mosbergen, Dominique, "Netflix, Ellen DeGeneres Are Making A 'Green Eggs And Ham' TV Series," *Huffington Post*, April 30, 2015, www.huffingtonpost.com/2015/04/30/green-eggs-and-ham-netflix-ellen-degeneres_n_7177182.html.

Page 87: TV News Desk, "Ellen DeGeneres Launches Seasonal Home Collection with QVC," October 15, 2014, www.prnewswire.com/news-releases/ellen-degeneres-launches-seasonal-home-collection-with-qvc-279310792.html.

Page 88: Petrilla, Molly, "Look out, Gwyneth: Ellen DeGeneres launches a lifestyle brand," *Fortune*, June 30, 2015, fortune.com/2015/06/30/ellen-degeneres-lifestyle-brand.

Page 90: Fleeman, Mike, "Ellen DeGeneres Replacing Paula Abdul on Idol," *People*, September 9, 2009, www.people.com/people/article/0,,20303396,00.html.

Page 90: Fleeman, "Ellen DeGeneres Replacing Paula Abdul on Idol."

Page 90: Collins, Scott, "Ellen DeGeneres Is Out as 'American Idol' Judge," *Los Angeles Times*, July 29, 2015, articles.latimes.com/2010/jul/29/entertainment/la-et-ellen-degeneres-american-idol.

GLOSSARY

abate To lessen, reduce, or remove.

activist A person who pushes for social change.

ag-gag law A law that prohibits undercover filming or photographing of farms without the owner's permission. These laws make it easier for operators to hide the abuse of the animals in their care.

anorexia An eating disorder that causes someone to refuse to eat in order to lose weight. Many anorexics believe they are fat, even if they are dangerously thin.

bit Part of a comedic act that focuses on a certain topic.

bulimia An eating disorder that causes someone to deliberately vomit after eating in order to lose weight. Like anorexics, many bulimics believe they are fat, even if they are dangerously thin.

Defense of Marriage Act (DOMA) A US law that denied federal benefits to same-sex couples. DOMA was overturned on June 26, 2013, paving the way for same-sex marriage nationwide.

distributor A company that is responsible for marketing a film or TV show.

emcee A person who performs as a master of ceremonies.

envoy A person on a diplomatic mission.

green card A permit that allows someone from a foreign country to permanently live and work in the United States.

heady Describes something that is exciting or exhilarating.

opener The person at a comedy club who warms up the audience.

producer A person who is in charge of creating a TV show or other type of production.

Proposition 8 A law in California that prohibited same-sex couples from marrying.

sitcom A comedic television show, which is a shortening of "situation comedy."

stay In judicial terms, the postponement of the implementation of a law or sentence.

trepidation A feeling of fear about what could happen next.

unconstitutional A law or action that is not in accordance with a country's constitution.

vegan A person who does not eat or use products made from animals.

FURTHER INFORMATION

Books

DeGeneres, Ellen. *My Point...And I Do Have One*. New York: Bantam, 1995.

————. *The Funny Thing Is*. New York: Simon & Schuster, 2004.

————. *Seriously...I'm Kidding*. New York: Grand Central Publishing, 2011.

Websites

The Ellen DeGeneres Show

www.EllenTV.com

The online home for *The Ellen DeGeneres Show* includes video clips, information about episodes, and giveaways.

Ellen DeGeneres on Facebook

www.facebook.com/EllenTV

Follow DeGeneres's Facebook feed here.

Ellen DeGeneres on Twitter

twitter.com/TheEllenShow

DeGeneres uses Twitter to keep in touch with fans.

Ellen DeGeneres on Instagram

www.instagram.com/theEllenshow

Instagram fans can follow DeGeneres here.

***People* Magazine Celebrity Central: Ellen DeGeneres**

www.people.com/people/ellen_degeneres/biography/

A brief bio of DeGeneres, with links to relevant articles.

Video

Ellen DeGeneres Funny First Appearance on Johnny Carson's Tonight Show

www.youtube.com/watch?v=YIAAI3j_vsY

Watch the routine that made DeGeneres famous: "Phone Call to God."

BIBLIOGRAPHY

"7 Amazing Graduation Commencement Speeches." *Goodnet*, May 23, 2013. http://www.goodnet.org/articles/7-amazing-graduation-commencement-speeches.

n.d. *Ag-gag*. Wikipedia. https://en.wikipedia.org/wiki/Ag-gag.

Billups, Andrea. "Ellen DeGeneres on Hosting the Academy Awards: 'It's Good to Do Something That Scares You'." *People*, March 1, 2014. http://www.peoplestylewatch.com/people/stylewatch/package/article/0,,20768377_20791947,00.html.

Brownfield, Paul. "'The First Time I Ever Had My Heart Broken.'" *Los Angeles Times*. September 16, 2001. http://articles.latimes.com/2001/sep/16/entertainment/ca-46244.

n.d. *California Proposition 8 (2008)*. Wikipedia. https://en.wikipedia.org/wiki/California_Proposition_8_(2008).

Capretto, Lisa. 2015. "How the Tragic Death of Ellen DeGeneres' Ex Changed Her Life." *Huffington Post*, October 26, 2015. http://www.huffingtonpost.com/entry/ellen-degeneres-ex-girlfriend-death_us_562a9a07e4b0443bb5640afc.

Carter, Bill. "At Lunch With: Ellen DeGeneres; Dialed God (Pause). He Laughed." *New York Times*, April 13, 1994. http://www.nytimes.com/1994/04/13/garden/at-lunch-with-ellen-degeneres-dialed-god-pause-he-laughed.html.

Chestang, Raphael. "EXCLUSIVE: Ellen DeGeneres Says 'Finding Nemo' Came Along at Her Lowest Point" *ET Online*, November 19, 2015. http://www.etonline.com/news/176466_exclusive_ellen_degeneres_says_finding_nemo_came_along_at_her_lowest_point.

Collins, Scott. "Ellen DeGeneres Is Out as 'American Idol' Judge." *Los Angeles Times*, July 29, 2010. http://articles.latimes.com/2010/jul/29/entertainment/la-et-ellen-degeneres-american-idol.

Davis, Caris. "Ellen DeGeneres Defends the Right of Gay Marriage." *People*, September 24, 2008. http://www.people.com/people/article/0,,20228501,00.html.

Dawn, Randee. Ellen DeGeneres brings wit, charm back to Oscars hosting gig. *Today*, March 1, 2014. http://www.today.com/popculture/ellen-degeneres-brings-wit-charm-back-oscars-hosting-gig-2D12164421.

DeGeneres, Ellen. *Home*. New York: Grand Central Publishing, 2015.

DeGeneres, Ellen. *My Point...And I Do Have One*. New York: Bantam Books, 1995.

DeGeneres, Ellen. *Phone Call to God*. Performed by Ellen DeGeneres. NBC TV West Coast Studios, Burbank, 1986.

DeGeneres, Ellen. *Seriously...I'm Kidding*. New York: Grand Central Publishing, 2011.

DeGeneres, Ellen, and Elizabeth Leonard. "Ellen DeGeneres on Life, the Oscars and Finding True Love." *People*, February 21, 2014. http://www.people.com/people/article/0,,20789294,00.html.

"Ellen DeGeneres named global envoy for AIDS awareness." *Reuters*, November 9, 2011. http://www.reuters.com/article/us-ellendegeneres-idUSTRE7A85O520111109.

"Ellen DeGeneres to Host 79th Academy Awards Presentation." Academy of Motion Picture Arts and Sciences, September 7, 2006. https://web.archive.org/web/20060929132634/http://www.oscars.org/press/pressreleases/2006/06.09.07.html .

"Ellen DeGeneres on DOMA & Prop 8 Rulings: 'It's a Supremely Wonderful Day'." *People*, June 26, 2013. http://www.people.com/people/article/0,,20712433,00.html.

Fleeman, Mike. "Ellen DeGeneres Replacing Paula Abdul on Idol." *People*, September 9, 2009. http://www.people.com/people/article/0,,20712433,00.html.

Foley, Bridget. "Ellen DeGeneres." *W*, March 2007. http://www.wmagazine.com/people/celebrities/2007/03/ellen_degeneres.

Foley, Bridget. "DeGeneres's Next Gig: Lifestyle Guru." *Women's Wear Daily*, July 8, 2014. http://wwd.com/fashion-news/fashion-features/ellens-next-gig-design-guru-7787209.

Gardner, Chris, and Ulrica Wihlborg. "DeGeneres's New Squeeze: Portia de Rossi." *People*, December 15, 2004. http://www.people.com/people/article/0,,1007643,00.html.

Gilman, Greg. "Ellen DeGeneres Returns as Oscar Host: 5 of Her Best Award Show Moments." *The Wrap*, August 3, 2013. http://www.thewrap.com/ellen-degeneres-returns-oscars-host-5-amazing-award-show-moments-video-108091.

Green, Jesse. "Come Out. Come Down. Come Back. Being Ellen DeGeneres." *New York Times Magazine*, August 19, 2001. http://www.nytimes.com/2001/08/19/magazine/come-out-come-down-come-back-being-ellen.html?pagewanted=all

Hall, Sarah. "Ellen DeGeneres Talks Abuse." *E! Online*, May 18, 2005. http://www.eonline.com/news/49889/ellen-degeneres-talks-abuse.

Hochman, David. "Ellen DeGeneres: Nice Girls Finish First." *Good Housekeeping*, September 10, 2011. http://www.goodhousekeeping.com/life/inspirational-stories/interviews/a18893/ellen-degeneres-interview.

Huver, Scott. "Portia de Rossi Is a Changed Woman Thanks to Marriage." *People*, January 17, 2009. http://www.people.com/people/article/0,,20253446,00.html.

Jordan, Julie. "Chatting With...DeGeneres & Portia." *People*, September 1, 2008. http://www.people.com/people/archive/article/0,,20221816,00.html.

Jordan, Julie. "Portia de Rossi: 'I Don't Want to Have Any More Secrets'." *People*, November 3, 2010. http://www.people.com/people/article/0,,20438754,00.html.

La Ferla, Ruth. "Like the Makeup Model, Warts and All?" *New York Times*, September 19, 2008. http://www.nytimes.com/2008/09/21/fashion/21ellen.html.

Lehner, Marla. "Ellen DeGeneres: I Was Molested." *People*, May 18, 2005. http://www.people.com/people/article/0,,1062732,00.html.

Mosbergen, Dominique. 2015. *Netflix, Ellen DeGeneres Are Making A 'Green Eggs And Ham' TV Series. Huffington Post*, April 30, 2015. http://www.huffingtonpost.com/2015/04/30/green-eggs-and-ham-netflix-ellen-degeneres_n_7177182.html.

n.d. *Mr. Wrong.* Wikipedia. https://en.wikipedia.org/wiki/Mr._Wrong.

Nudd, Tim. "Ellen DeGeneres: Portia Is 'My Perfect Fit'." *People*, January 27, 2007. http://www.people.com/people/article/0,,20009962,00.html.

Park, Andrea. "Just Keep Swimming! Ellen DeGeneres Reveals the First Trailer for Nemo Sequel Finding Dory." *People*, November 10, 2015. http://www.people.com/article/finding-dory-ellen-degeneres-releases-first-trailer-nemo-sequel.

Perkoff, Rachel (director). *Another Lost Angel, 2008.*

Petrilla, Molly. "Look out, Gwyneth: Ellen DeGeneres launches a lifestyle brand." *Fortune*, June 30, 2015. http://fortune.com/2015/06/30/ellen-degeneres-lifestyle-brand.

Phillips, Stone. "Catching Up with Ellen DeGeneres." *Dateline*, November 8, 2004. http://www.nbcnews.com/id/6430100/ns/dateline_nbc-newsmakers/t/catching-ellen-degeneres.

Rabens, Chandler. "DeGeneres Uncensored." *Teen People*, February, 2006.

Rocca, Mo. 2012. *Ellen DeGeneres: My Job's to Make You Happy.* CBS News, June 12, 2012.

Rothman, Michael. Ellen DeGeneres Reveals the Negatives that Happened After Coming Out. *ABC News*, October 27, 2015. http://abcnews.go.com/Entertainment/ellen-degeneres-reveals-negatives-happened-coming/story?id=34764473.

Saad, Nardine. "Ellen DeGeneres rides tidal wave of excitement over 'Finding Dory'." *Los Angeles Times*, April 3, 2013. http://articles.latimes.com/2013/apr/03/entertainment/la-et-mg-ellen-degeneres-finding-dory-20130403.

Schwarzbaum, Lisa. *My Point...And I Do Have One. Entertainment Weekly*, September 8, 2008. http://www.ew.com/article/1995/09/08/book-review-my-point-and-i-do-have-one.

Silverman, Stephen M. "Ellen DeGeneres Reacts to Gay Marriage Ban." *People*, November 6, 2008. http://www.people.com/people/article/0,,20238579,00.html.

Silverman, Steven M. "Ellen DeGeneres Helped Mom with Cancer Fight." *People*, September 27, 2007. http://www.people.com/people/article/0,,20058779,00.html.

Smith, Michael. "Ellen DeGeneres the Delicious Irony of Hosting Oscar Ceremony Again." *Liberty Voice*, August 3, 2013. http://guardianlv.com/2013/08/DeGeneres-degeneres-the-delicious-irony-of-hosting-oscar-ceremony-again.

Smolowe, Jill. "Yep, It's Over." *People*. September 4, 2000. http://www.people.com/people/archive/article/0,,20132187,00.html.

Tracy, Kathleen. *Ellen The Real Story of Ellen DeGeneres*. Secaucus, NJ: Carol Publishing Group, 1999.

TV News Desk. "Ellen DeGeneres Launches Seasonal Home Collection with QVC." *PR Newswire*, October 15, 2014. http://www.prnewswire.com/news-releases/ellen-degeneres-launches-seasonal-home-collection-with-qvc-279310792.html.

"Wry Toast." *People*, July 19, 1999. http://www.people.com/people/archive/article/0,,20128761,00.html.

INDEX

ABOUT THE AUTHOR

Kate Shoup has authored more than thirty books on a variety of topics and has edited scores more. For Cavendish Square, Kate's titles include *Serena Williams, Kate Middleton, Billie Jean King, Texas and the Mexican War, The California Gold Rush, Life as a Soldier in the Civil War, Life as an Engineer on the First Railroads of America, Life as a Prospector in the California Gold Rush, Egypt, India, Greece,* and *Rohypnol.* Kate has also co-written a feature-length screenplay (and starred in the ensuing film) and worked as the Sports Editor for *NUVO Newsweekly.* When not writing, Kate, an IndyCar fanatic, loves to ski, read, and ride her motorcycle. She lives in Indianapolis with her husband, her daughter, and their dog.